MW00625329

In *Losing Yourself a... . ...a...g ,.,,,* ....
job with combining raw and real with a biblical perspective.
True joy cannot come by our own strength, might, power,
nor knowledge. True joy only comes from Christ. Michelle
does an easy-to-understand, yet in-depth study of Jonah, a
man well known for his encounter with being in the belly of
a whale. As I read this book, I remembered the many times
I've wandered and was in desperate need of having my path
straightened or restored. Christ did exactly that by helping
me lose myself and He can do the same for you! We are all
broken people in need of Someone to fix us. Michelle's book
will help you by pointing you to the One and Only True
Restorer.

—*JudyLynn Cabal, host of the Making Today Matter Podcast
and blogger at makingtodaymatter.com*

Michelle may be quiet in personality, but she has a mighty
pen that speaks words of wisdom. I appreciate her transpar-
ency as she shares lessons that God has taught her. She has
been a good student and learned well from her Teacher. I
love that she has a passion to share with her readers so they
too can experience the riches found in God's Word. This
study on Jonah is insightful and will help anyone with an
open heart to grow in their love for God and their trust in
Him. Michelle has a deep desire to help people, and this
book will be of help to you!

—*Suza Rasmussen, Instructor at West Coast Baptist College*

Friends offer fresh perspective by sharing ideas with their own unique insights. Michelle does this in her book *Losing Yourself and Finding Joy.* She shines a light on the book of Jonah and teaches us about selflessness and God's goodness. The blend of interesting personal stories, Scripture references, and teaching make for a fascinating read. In these pages you will find a fresh view of the book of Jonah that will cause you to examine your own life. I highly recommend it!

—*Kassie Selby, writer at juneandjoyblog.com*

Losing Yourself & Finding Joy

JONAH, GOD'S WAYWARD PROPHET

MICHELLE ELAINE BURTON

Michelle Elaine Burton
Philippians 2:5-7

www.michelleelaineburton.com

Cover & interior designed by Typewriter Creative Co.
Cover photo by Emre on Unsplash.com

All Scripture quotations are taken from the King James Version.

The author has put forth every effort to give proper credit to quotes and thoughts that are not original with the author. It is not the intent of the author to claim originality with any quote or thought that could not readily be tied to an original source.

FIRST EDITION

ISBN 978-1-7360079-2-1 (Paperback)
ISBN 978-1-7360079-3-8 (eBook)

*For my mom, who modeled to me
what true Joy looks like.*

CONTENTS

INTRODUCTION

I can hear the echo of my mom's voice in my mind, all these years later.

"Michelle, you don't have a lot of joy in your life. Remember, 'JOY' is spelled Jesus, Others, You."

She said this to me countless times growing up, and it's a lesson I'm still learning. My mom's name is Joy, and true joy exudes from her in an almost visible way. Many have commented on how aptly named she is. And she really does know the secret of joy; her life is marked by serving God first, serving others second, and putting herself last. She has sacrificed herself for me more times than I can count. She had every right to admonish me to follow her as she followed Christ over the years when she watched me struggle to have true joy, struggle to put anyone above myself. Often her admonition was followed with this statement:

"You have a whole lot of 'Jesus' in your life, and a whole lot of 'You.' But not much 'Others.'"

It was true. At least, from the outside it seemed to

be true. I read my Bible every day, and I was involved in every church activity you could imagine. But to be honest, even that was about me when I was a teenager. I wanted to have the appearance of being someone spiritual. And I did a good job fooling many people.

When I finally accepted Christ at the age of nineteen, I was able to learn to truly put Jesus first in my life. I learned how to have a deep and fulfilling relationship with Him, to truly serve Him because He is worthy, not because I want others to think well of me. But that whole thing about "others?" Somehow that one's still hard for me.

I like my alone time. And I don't like for it to be interrupted. I schedule my days in a meticulously organized day planner, and I struggle to not be annoyed if I'm asked to change my plans in any way. If you want me to do something, you should give me at least a week's notice. But true joy is never found in this "me first" mentality; true joy is found in putting myself last.

When God showed me that the topic of this book was to be selflessness, I think I nearly passed out in my chair. Last week when I went home from my writing day, I was completely convinced that I would not be able to finish this book; I still have way too much to learn about putting others before myself. Having a toddler gives me daily practice, but I still feel the monster of selfishness rising up at times when I'm trying to meet her needs.

Last Friday night, I was up with my daughter at midnight, just like I am many nights. I felt the frustration beginning to rise. Why wouldn't she just sleep? I stumbled into the living room in the dark without even bothering to put my glasses on. I opened my laptop and squinted at the bright screen. I tried to muster up every bit of courage within me to delete the thousands of words I had already written for this book. After all, how could I be such a hypocrite as to write a book on selflessness?

I didn't delete my work. Instead of giving up on writing, I surrendered to God. It was time for me to overcome a besetting sin in my life. And for some reason, God wanted me to take all of you along on the journey as well. It's time for all of us to learn together to put ourselves last.

But if I always put myself last, how will I be taken care of? Who will meet my needs?

There's a prophet in the Bible who I believe must have struggled with these questions as well. He claimed to serve God, but he struggled to put others before himself time and time again. And the lack of true joy in his life is striking. I want to invite you to take a walk through the story of Jonah with me. Perhaps you can lose yourself and find joy along the way.

chapter one

WHEN GOD SAYS, "GO."

I'd rather stay,
But God says, "Go."
Come what may,
I will do so.

As I sit on the old leather sofa on the second floor of my favorite coffee shop, I can't help but laugh at myself, knowing what I'm about to tell you. My husband, Steven, encouraged me to go out today; he knows there's a message stirring in my heart, and he believes it's worth the investment of my time to put that message on paper.

He's been preparing me for this day all week: *"On Friday, I'm going to stay home with Angela, and you're going to go out and write."*

I've been resisting all week.

"I don't need to go out."

"I don't want to have to drive anywhere."

"I can just write at home while she naps."

To say that I'm a homebody would be an understatement. There's a lot of good that comes from being at home. I love homemaking, and I believe that it's an art. I want to make my home the most comfortable and wonderful place to be in the world for myself and for my family. Growth can happen at home on all sorts of levels. But I believe some of God's greatest work in my life has transpired when I stepped out of that comfort zone of home and followed His leading into the unknown. I think that a man named Jonah would tell you the same thing.

Jonah was a prophet in Israel during the reign of King Jeroboam. God appointed prophets to bring His message to His people, so the book of Jonah naturally begins with God giving a message to His prophet, Jonah.

Jonah 1:1-2
Now the word of the Lord came unto Jonah the son of Amittai, saying, Arise, go to Nineveh, that great city, and cry against it; for their wickedness is come up before me.

Nineveh, located in modern day Iraq, was a city known for its wickedness. But God had a message for them, and His chosen man to deliver that message was Jonah. So, He called Jonah to leave his hometown of

Gath-hepher and travel over five hundred miles to that wicked city. They needed to know that they were sinners. They needed to have the chance to repent.

What a daunting task! I can't imagine the fear and trepidation that Jonah must have felt. I hardly wanted to leave my home to go write in a quiet place today; in the times that God asks me to go farther, my heart usually sinks to my stomach. I would rather stay, but many times God has asked me to go.

When I was eighteen, He asked me to leave my home in Tennessee to go to college in California; I resisted. But that's where I came to know Him as my Savior.

Sometimes when God asks us to go, it comes in the form of a seeming adventure. It seems easier to go in those times. When God asked me to follow the husband He gave me to Utah, I happily followed. I didn't know that that's where He would grow me through trials and troubles. But it's also where He blessed us with a daughter, our greatest joy in life.

Then God asked me to go somewhere I never imagined He would: back to my hometown in Chattanooga, Tennessee. The request came in the form of a letter from my former Spanish teacher who is the pastor of Life Gate Baptist Church. I was home by myself with our one-month-old baby when the letter came, and when I saw the return address I opened it immediately. I expected a letter congratulating us on the birth of our daughter, and that was part of the letter. But the real purpose of the letter knocked the wind out of me. Pastor Dunn wrote that the Lord had put it on his heart to ask Steven and me to come work with the teens at his church and be involved in outreach ministry. I spent the rest of the day sitting in my comfy chair holding my new baby, transfixed by absolute horror at the thought of moving to Tennessee.

When my husband came home and saw the look on my face, he thought someone had died. When I showed him the letter, I was surprised to see that he was actually happy about the prospect of moving. What an exciting possible next step God had for us! He had already learned the lesson that I was still resisting: when God says, "Go," His way is best.

The next several months were spent in prayer and in communication with Pastor Dunn. We probably would have made our decision much sooner if I hadn't been so intent on resisting God's clear leading in our lives. I didn't want to go! I was comfortable right where I was, thank you very much. How was I supposed to know if this was God's leading when I didn't feel peace? And how was I supposed to feel peace when I didn't want to leave the only home our little family of three had ever known?

Steven had begun to feel great peace about moving. And God brought me back to this one thought: my calling had not changed. My calling was to follow my husband and help him in whatever ministry the Lord had him in. So if God was calling Steven to Chattanooga, Tennessee, He was calling me too.

I wish I could say that I came to that conclusion joyfully. It took five months for me to get to that point, and then it took another four months for us to actually be able to make the move. When the day of our move came, there wasn't a hint of a smile on my face. Our parents had come to help us make the long move, and as our caravan set out to make the trek back to Tennessee, I couldn't help but see a stark contrast with our move to Utah three and a half years earlier.

We had set out as newlyweds with all our belongings in a brightly colored U-Haul with a painting of a viking ship on the side. We were rested from a full night of sleep and full of hope for the future. I expressed aloud for the first time my desire to write a book, and my new husband eagerly supported my dream. We arrived in Utah in the middle of a beautiful snowy winter, and my husband carried his new bride over the threshold of our first apartment.

When we made the return journey that we never imagined making, we set out in a plain yellow Penske truck followed by our two cars. Our belongings had somehow multiplied, and every square inch of space was packed to the brim. Some of that space was taken up by our ten-month-old baby and her belongings; some was occupied by our two hamsters. Our sleep the night before had been broken as usual since we had become parents, and we were exhausted. I had a finished manuscript on my laptop and no idea what to do with it. It seemed like our original dreams were all falling apart. We arrived in Tennessee in the middle of a hot and humid summer, and moved the bare minimum of our belongings into my parents' house where we stayed while we looked for a place of our own. My husband was full of hope, but I was still a little skeptical. Was it really true that God had a good plan for us here?

Mark 9:24
...Lord, I believe; help Thou mine unbelief!

In the short time that we've been in Tennessee, I can already see God's hand of blessing. He provided the perfect home for us, a little two bedroom duplex with an amazing garage for my husband to pursue his interest in woodworking. He connected me with the people who taught me how to publish my book, and four months after our move, I had the first printed copy in my hands. The blessing of our daughter being able to grow up near her grandparents has been unspeakably beautiful. Not to mention how immediately connected we felt with our new church — it was like coming home to a place we had never been before.

Perhaps one of the best blessings has been the ability to spend time with my grandparents. When we moved back, all four of my grandparents were still living in town. Seeing them on a regular basis and watching them enjoy their great-granddaughter has been a highlight of our days. Less than six months after we moved, my Papaw went to heaven. What a gift God gave me in being able to spend time with him those last few months, to have one last Thanksgiving and one last Christmas Eve, to watch my daughter play ball with him in their den, and grow to love him as he always loved all of us with his whole heart.

That last Christmas Eve with Papaw is a memory I will treasure forever. Christmas Eve at Mimi and Papaw's house was one of my most cherished childhood traditions. I had missed it for three years while we were living in Utah, but when we moved back to Tennessee, we were excited to rejoin the tradition with our little family of three. It was different than we expected though. Papaw had suffered from many health issues over the years, but in the weeks before Christmas, he had declined quickly. He was a shell of himself that night, but he was there. I'm sure he was smiling for our sakes; he was always thinking of his family, putting aside his own pain. As we said our goodbyes that evening, I told Papaw I would call on Tuesday, just as I always did. He smiled and hugged me, and the weakness in his body was striking in comparison to the strong man he had once been. He hugged and kissed Angela, and she blew kisses in return as she waved goodbye. Later that evening, Papaw was taken to the hospital. The day after Christmas, God took him to heaven. Did God know what He was doing when He moved us here at the time that He did? Absolutely.

It's always easier to stay than it is to go, but the blessings come when we get into motion. I'm going to make my mechanical engineer brother proud for a moment and attempt to give you a science lesson. (Or I may completely embarrass him. We'll see.) Newton's first law of motion says that an object at rest will stay at rest, and an object in motion will stay in motion unless it's acted upon by an external force. This applies to the physical universe, and I believe it applies to us spiritually as well.

It's so much easier to stay at rest; it's our nature to be comfortable right where we are. But when God calls us to action, blessing and reward are found in motion. When I returned home from my first afternoon writing at the coffee shop, I thanked my husband for encouraging me to go, even when I had protested. His response was, "We all need a little push sometimes." There's that first law of motion, the need to be acted upon by an external force. Little did Jonah know how much of a push into God's calling He was soon to receive.

QUESTIONS FOR DISCUSSION

1. At what times in your life has God told you to go?

2. When God has told you to go, have you resisted or followed willingly?

3. What blessings have you found when you have followed God's leading?

4. Are you a little too comfortable where you are right now? If God called you to go, would you be willing?

chapter Two

THE PRESENCE
OF THE LORD

I can run from God's will,
But from His presence I cannot.
He loves me still,
And I'm in His every thought.

Sometimes I just want to be alone. As an extreme introvert, I need quiet time to think, reflect, and process. This is how God made me. Jonah took his desire to be alone to a completely different level.

Jonah 1:3
But Jonah rose up to flee unto Tarshish from the presence of the Lord, and went down to Joppa; and he found a ship going to Tarshish: so he paid the fare thereof, and went down into it, to go with them unto Tarshish from the presence of the Lord.

Jonah decided that he most certainly did *not* want to go to Nineveh. I mean, are you kidding me? Those people didn't deserve to hear God's message of forgiveness! And even if they did, Jonah was not going to put his life at risk to tell them. As far as he was concerned, the most likely outcome was that he would be killed. Although fear of the Ninevites likely played a part in Jonah's disobedience, he tells us himself later in the book his biggest reason for not wanting to go: he knew God was merciful. He knew that God would forgive the Ninevites. And He didn't want that to happen. Jonah's thoughts and affections were devoted to himself and to his people, the Israelites. There was no way he was going to sacrifice himself for these people who were the enemies of the Jews. So, instead of making the over five hundred mile journey to Nineveh, he instead made the sixty mile journey to Joppa. There he found a ship going to Tarshish, more than 2,500 miles in the opposite direction from his God-ordained destination of Nineveh. He was going to get away from everything and everyone, including the presence of God.

Jonah wasn't the first to make a futile attempt at hiding from God's presence. The first people to do this were actually the first people on this earth: Adam and Eve. When Eve took of the forbidden fruit and shared with her husband, Adam, they recognized their sin and shame. Their immediate response was to try to hide from God's presence.

Genesis 3:8
And they heard the voice of the Lord God walking in the garden in the cool of the day: and Adam and his wife hid themselves from the presence of the Lord God amongst the trees of the garden.

They quickly learned that it was impossible to hide from God's presence.

Genesis 3:9
And the Lord God called unto Adam and said unto him, Where art thou?

Keep in mind, God knew exactly where they were, but His desire was for them to come to Him, even in their newly fallen state.

Genesis 3:10-11
And he said, I heard thy voice in the garden, and I was afraid, because I was naked: and I hid myself. And he said, Who told thee that thou wast naked? Hast thou eaten of the tree, whereof I commanded thee that thou shouldest not eat?

God knew what they had done. He knew that they had eaten of the forbidden fruit. Yet He was giving them a chance to confess.

Genesis 3:12-13
And the man said, The woman whom thou gavest to be with me, she gave me of the tree, and I did

eat. And the Lord God said unto the woman, What
is this that thou hast done? And the woman said,
The serpent beguiled me, and I did eat.

Thus began the blame game. However, casting blame on others did not take away the consequences for what they had done, nor did attempting to hide from God's presence. God, even in His giving of the punishment that was deserved, gave a promise for redemption.

Genesis 3:14-15
And the Lord God said unto the serpent, Because
thou hast done this, thou art cursed above all cat-
tle, and above every beast of the field: upon thy bel-
ly shalt thou go, and dust shalt thou eat all the days
of thy life: and I will put enmity between thee and
the woman, and between thy seed and her seed; it
shall bruise thy head, and thou shalt bruise his heel.

"Her seed" in this verse is the first reference to the coming of Jesus. Jesus was the only person ever born who was not the seed of a man, but of a virgin woman. Even in the aftermath of their sin, God was already planning their redemption. They didn't need to hide from God's presence; even in their sin, they could have run to Him. He was ready to forgive.

Job is another character who wished he could somehow get away from God's presence.

Job 7:14-19

When I say, My bed shall comfort me, my couch shall ease my complaint; then thou scarest me with dreams, and terrifiest me through visions: so that my soul chooseth strangling, and death rather than my life. I loathe it; I would not live alway: let me alone; for my days are vanity. What is man that thou shouldest visit him every morning, and try him every moment? How long wilt thou not depart from me, nor let me alone till I swallow down my spittle?

In Job's case, he had done nothing wrong, but it seemed to him that God was pouring out His wrath on him. He had lost everything he had, and he was done with it all. He had come to the point that he felt life was futile, and if he couldn't die, he at least wanted to get away from the God that seemed He no longer cared. He cried out, "Let me alone!" It seemed that he couldn't even get away from God long enough to swallow his own spit. But this was not his final conclusion; once he had wrestled with his doubts, he came to a place where he was willing to trust God, regardless of his circumstances.

Job 19:25-27

For I know that my redeemer liveth, and that he shall stand at the latter day upon the earth: and though after my skin worms destroy this body, yet

in my flesh shall I see God: whom I shall see for my-
self, and mine eyes shall behold, and not another;
though my reins be consumed within me.

The psalmist, David, finally addressed this futility of hiding from God's presence.

Psalm 139:7-11
Whither shall I go from thy spirit? or whither shall
I flee from thy presence? If I ascend up into heav-
en, thou art there: if I make my bed in hell, behold,
thou art there. If I take the wings of the morning,
and dwell in the uttermost parts of the sea; even
there shall thy hand lead me and thy right hand
shall hold me. If I say, Surely the darkness shall
cover me; even the night shall be light about me.

David acknowledged that there was no getting
away from God's presence, but perhaps that was a
good thing. When times are tough, it may seem that
God has forgotten. We may wish to get away from Him
because we perceive that He has somehow wronged
us. But He is the one who will lead us through the valley and hold us in the darkness if we will let Him. And
when He calls us to get out of our comfort zones like
Jonah? He'll be there in those moments too.

When I walked through my darkest valley of losing our first child ten weeks into my pregnancy, I just
wanted to be alone. I was afraid of the insensitive

comments others would make; I didn't want to deal with the pain. So I ignored it. I was tempted to try to hide from God as well, but I knew that I needed Him. I kept praying, and I kept seeking Him. I boldly asked Him for another baby. It was shortly after He answered those prayers that I decided that maybe it was in my best interest to distance myself from God a little bit.

On Christmas morning, I surprised my husband with the news that we were expecting another baby. We went forward with the confidence that God had answered our prayers, and we fully believed we would get to bring this baby home. However, two weeks later I was diagnosed with a blood clot in my womb that threatened to take the life of our second baby. I requested prayer from everyone I knew, but never once did I pray for healing for myself. It seemed to me that everything I asked God, He was doing the opposite.

I asked Him to spare the life of our first child; He took her to heaven anyway.

I asked Him to give us another child; it seemed unlikely that we would get to bring this baby home.

What would happen if I asked Him to heal me? Certainly He would do the exact opposite. So I stopped praying for things for myself, fearing what the outcome would be. In time, I stopped praying altogether. I just wanted God to leave me alone.

In spite of my lack of faith, He did heal me from that blood clot, and He did allow our second daughter,

Angela, to be born full term and completely healthy. But repairing my relationship with God took quite some time. He had not changed; He was right there waiting for me. I was the one who had changed. I was the one who had strayed.

After Angela was born, my prayers started out as scattered, desperate pleas for help when I needed it most. My friend Priscilla calls these "vending machine prayers." I don't know how to describe them better than she does, so I'm going to share her words with you here.

Have you ever heard people say something about how sometimes we treat God like a vending machine? Like He's there to give us anything we ask for at that moment, and when He doesn't give us what we want, we get frustrated as if He's not doing His job? I call those prayers "vending machine prayers." And, though I know I've been guilty of them throughout my entire life, I feel like since I've had my daughter, I've gotten worse about them. Especially around bedtime. I find myself constantly praying things like, "God, please let her stay sleeping when I lay her down. Lord, you know I am SO tired, and I just need some me time," or something along those lines. And while that prayer isn't necessarily "bad," I know that, for me personally, very often when I'm praying it I'm praying out of a

*selfish heart. I also know that I'm usually praying
and responding with some sass when He doesn't
answer how I want right away. It's definitely something I'm working on.*

God wants us to come to Him with our most immediate needs, but He doesn't want our relationship
with Him to stop at that. He wants to be intimate with
us. As I began to repair my relationship with the Lord,
slowly my prayers turned into more bold attempts at
talking to the One who loves me the most. It was over
a year after my daughter was born that I started calling
God "Father" again, truly pursuing a personal relationship with Him. But even when I was trying to hide, He
was there.

Jeremiah 23:23-24
*Am I a God at hand, saith the Lord, and not a God
afar off? Can any hide himself in secret places that
I shall not see him? saith the Lord. Do not I fill
heaven and earth? saith the Lord.*

What good did it do to try to run from God's presence? He was there all along anyway. Hiding from the
One who could heal me only caused me more grief
than I needed to bear.

Jonah would soon learn of the grief that comes
from hiding from the One who longed to lead him and
guide him, even into the spiritual darkness of Nineveh.

QUESTIONS FOR DISCUSSION

1. Have you ever tried to somehow hide from God's presence?

2. Whom do you relate with the most:

    - Adam and Eve, hiding from God in their sin?

    - Job, hiding from God in the midst of his trial?

    - Jonah, hiding from God when he didn't want to do His will?

3. What is your prayer life like? Are you only praying "vending machine prayers," or do you have a truly intimate relationship with God?

chapter Three

PAYING THE FARE

Sin will cost me more
Than I ever want to pay,
But grace can restore
When there seems to be no way.

"Sin will take you farther than you want to go, keep you longer than you want to stay, and cost you more than you want to pay."

Although it is unknown where this exact quote originated, my mother said it often when we were children. I've remembered it because it's catchy, but the truth of it has delved deeper into my heart over the years as I have learned some things the hard way and watched this play out in the lives of others over and over again.

Jonah 1:3
But Jonah rose up to flee unto Tarshish from the presence of the Lord, and went down to Joppa; and he found a ship going to Tarshish: so he paid the fare thereof, and went down into it, to go with them unto Tarshish from the presence of the Lord.

Jonah would have to pay a price for his choice to flee from God's presence, and paying the fare for his ride to Tarshish was just the beginning. Yet he wasn't the only person mentioned in the Bible who paid a price for the choice to disobey God.

During his earthly ministry, Jesus told a story that we usually refer to as "the prodigal son." You may be familiar with it: a man had two sons, and his younger son wanted his inheritance *now.* So, his father did what his son wanted. And the son did whatever his wicked heart desired.

Luke 15:13
And not many days after the youngest son gathered all together, and took his journey into a far country, and there wasted his substance with riotous living.

Riotous means, "marked by or involving public disorder; characterized by wild and uncontrolled behavior." He did whatever he wanted, with no regard to morality. He had no care for what the consequences might be, but as they always do, the consequences came.

Luke 15:14
And when he had spent all, there arose a mighty
famine in that land; and he began to be in want.

A famine came to the land, meaning food was scarce. He had spent all that he had, and the "friends" he had spent his time with certainly didn't want anything to do with him now that his money was gone. He was at a complete loss.

Luke 15:15-16
And he went and joined himself to a citizen of
that country; and he sent him into his fields to
feed swine. And he would fain have filled his belly
with the husks that the swine did eat: and no man
gave unto him.

He found some work to do, albeit dirty work. Feeding pigs certainly isn't how this son of a wealthy Jewish man imagined he would spend his days. Pigs were an unclean animal to the Jews; spending his time with pigs would have been degrading and humiliating. His debasement went a step farther. "Fain" isn't a word we use much anymore, but it means, "with pleasure; gladly." He was in such want that he was glad to eat the slop that the pigs were eating. Sin had taken him much farther than he ever wanted to go.

I think of Lot, Abraham's nephew. He was following Abraham as God led him, but there came a point in the journey where the land was physically not able to contain their livestock. This wasn't a problem; they would simply divide the land between themselves so that there was no question of where their livestock should graze. Abraham gave Lot first pick, and he chose the land that looked best to him. This choice was not wrong. His mistake came when he pitched his tent.

Genesis 13:12-13
Abraham dwelled in the land of Canaan, and Lot dwelled in the cities of the plain, and pitched his tent toward Sodom. But the men of Sodom were wicked and sinners before the Lord exceedingly.

Something about this wicked city of Sodom caught Lot's attention. He pitched his tent towards it. He set his focus on it. And slowly that attraction grew. Right after these verses, the Bible tells a story of kings going to war. This is another story for another day, but Lot was captured in that war. We read something interesting regarding his capture.

Genesis 14:12
And they took Lot, Abram's brother's son, who dwelt in Sodom, and his goods, and departed.

What? Wait a minute. I thought he just pitched his tent facing Sodom? Somewhere along the way, the allure of this wicked city was more than he could resist. He chose to make his dwelling there. He had a family there. How did he go from following Abraham, and in turn following God, to living in a city known for its wickedness? God told Abraham that he was going to destroy Sodom, and Abraham pleaded for God to spare the life of his nephew, Lot. God would not spare the city because He could not even find ten righteous people there. But in His mercy, He did choose to spare Lot and his family. He sent two angels to Sodom for that exact purpose.

> *Genesis 19:1*
> *And there came two angels to Sodom at even; and Lot sat in the gate of Sodom: and Lot seeing them rose up to meet them; and he bowed himself with his face toward the ground;*

In the cultural context of that day, someone who "sat in the gate" of a city was on the city council. Somewhere along the way, Lot had gone from living with his tent facing Sodom, to living in Sodom, to being someone of great importance in that wicked city. How did he end up there? It started with his choice to keep sin right in front of his eyes. Lot had likely only planned to be separated from Abraham for a season out of the necessity for more space for his flocks. But sin had kept him away from God longer than he had ever intended to stay.

We've already talked about Adam and Eve. They made the choice to disobey the only command God had given them, not to eat of the forbidden fruit. God had told them that the cost for disobedience would be death. But I don't know if they understood the full extent of all that death entailed. Not only would they physically die, but everyone else born into the world after them would also physically die. With physical death, separation from the body, came the penalty of spiritual death, eternal separation from God. God would have to send His own Son to die a horrible bodily death in order to reverse the consequences of their disobedience. But not everyone would accept His substitutionary death. Many would still die and be separated from God eternally. Adam and Eve's sin cost far more than they wanted to pay.

I don't want to paint a completely dark picture in telling these stories. None of us can go farther than the reach of God's mercy and grace. In the story of the prodigal son, his father (who is a picture of God) welcomed him home with open arms. In the book of 2 Peter, Lot is called "just" and "righteous." God knew the true state of Lot's heart even if his actions didn't back it up, and He chose to spare him. God loved Adam and Eve so much that He sent His Son, Jesus, to pay the price for their sin. Jesus has paid the price for your sin and mine as well. There is forgiveness. There is redemption. But there are still consequences.

Proverbs 14:12
There is a way which seemeth right unto a man,
but the end thereof are the ways of death.

Although sin can take us farther than we want to go, keep us longer than we want to stay, and cost us more than we want to pay, there is always a way of escape. There's always a chance to make a change before it's too late.

1 Corinthians 10:13
There hath no temptation taken you but such as is common to man: but God is faithful, who will not suffer you to be tempted above that ye are able; but will with the temptation also make a way to escape, that ye may be able to bear it.

Over the last few years, I have had the privilege of watching God do an incredible work in the life of my friend Christina. Her testimony is one of God's forgiveness and redemption. I asked her if she would be willing to share her story with you. I know that God is receiving glory through her life, and I pray that her story will breathe hope into your life, no matter how far you have strayed.

If I didn't know that God has a plan for every one of us, I'd say that I was the result of a mistake. My mother and father were a dysfunctional young couple that tried to mend a relationship by having a baby. Soon after I was conceived, that relationship ended and my mother packed her bags to drive to the closest state where abortions were legal, but was unable to follow through with her intentions. Six months after I came into the world, I was dropped off at my father's parents' house, and from that moment on I was left to the responsibility of my young father and his parents.

Drugs and alcohol had been in my family's history on both sides, so my grandparents were determined to break the cycle when they took responsibility for me. My guardians banded together and sacrificed to send me to a Christian school. They changed their whole lives for the chance of creating a better life for me. By the age of three, I was reciting the books of the Bible, Psalm 23, and Psalm 100 in front of our church's congregation. Everyone was so proud of me. I felt a sense of responsibility to live up to the pedestal that I was put on in breaking the cycle. I was faithful in going to church every time the doors were open, I had accepted the Lord into my heart, I was an honors student, and I truly wanted to be an example for others because I knew it was no mistake that I had been spared. To others, it seemed that I was the poster child for perseverance. I had a desire to influence others and participated in multiple mission trips, was an active youth group leader, and sang in the church choir.

Despite all of this, I saw firsthand what substance

abuse resulted in. My dad and I shared a room when I was young, and he was in and out of jail a few times throughout my youth. When I was around the age of fifteen, my dad moved out to pursue a relationship. Seeing that I did not have a relationship with my mother, I was frequently worried about my dad's wellbeing. I struggled with abandonment and insecurity. I was incredibly angry that he left knowing that I was also abandoned by my mother. This anger, sadness, and hurt took over my life.

Soon after he moved out, I started seeing my first boyfriend. As I look back over the course of my life, this was my first true fork in the road, and I didn't even realize it. I remember thinking, "Why is this happening to me? I have been through so much already. I have done my best to persevere, but here I am in the driveway of my home crying on the ground begging my dad not to leave me. How could this be happening to me?" I faced an internal battle, as deep down I knew that the right decision was to pour myself into our Father in Heaven, but I sought earthly love and acceptance so deeply that I instead tried to find it in the boy I was dating.

Because I had become bitter with God for seemingly neglecting me and allowing me to go through so much pain after I felt I had worked so hard, I sought solace in the boy I was dating who I eventually gave myself to. Through this action, I chose which path to take, and after that I felt like there was no going back. I felt like everyone knew what I had done when I went to school the next day.

I felt ruined because I knew the right thing to do, but I still disregarded God's guidance.

Rather than submitting to the Lord, seeking forgiveness, and turning away from my sin, I ran farther and farther from God at this point, and the boy I was dating left me for someone else. I kept everything together on the outside and went on to be the first one in my family to graduate high school. I pretended that I was okay on the outside, but inside there was a storm brewing full of anger, regret, and shame as I went on to start college.

At this point in my mind, I was already a fraud. Everyone had an idea of me that was not accurate, so I felt I had to take it all the way. I worried about my image rather than my relationship with God. Because of my regret and shame, I gravitated towards people that didn't care about doing the right thing. I started dabbling in marijuana, and I thought it was dumb that everyone called this the "gateway drug." This wasn't a big deal; I thought I had everything under control. Everyone else was being irrational. I started smoking cigarettes and drinking heavily and growing my network of people that did the same. I showed no respect for my body, and sex was no big deal to me. My grandparents found out that I was living this way, so I stopped talking to them because I didn't want to hear what they had to say. I started being vocal about what I was doing on social media, and it was no secret that I had started my rebellion as I had multiple piercings on my face. I wanted to do whatever I could do to push people away that would try to get me to stop living my life this way. Eventually I started using drugs other than weed, I had lost over thirty pounds, and I was covered in tattoos at this point. The farther away I got from God, the less guilty I felt. When I did experience even an ounce of guilt, I covered it up with more drugs or alcohol.

After being an honors student in high school and earning a full scholarship to college, I failed all of my classes my freshman year and lost my scholarships after my whole family was so proud of me for being a first generation high school graduate.

This was a bit of a wake up call. I pulled it together just enough to start passing my classes but kept living this way. I was in a couple of relationships and would straighten up, and during the last two years of college I actually made the dean's list every semester and cleaned up my life substantially. But I never did it for God or for myself.

I knew God was always there, but I still pushed this out of my mind. Throughout this time in my life there were gentle whispers offering for me to come home to the Lord, but I figured I had it together "enough." After all, I was about to graduate college after completely failing, I had been in a relationship for a couple of years, and I had signed a contract with a Fortune 500 company that I would start working at after I graduated college. Looking back, I did pray now and again. I thanked God for allowing me to live through the times when drugs and alcohol nearly took my life on a couple of occasions. I thanked

God for the blessings in my life, but I took all of His chances and protection for granted. In a sense, this made me feel untouchable that I had made it so far after hitting rock bottom. Because of that feeling, I kept partying and living my life how I had in the past, but just enough to where I could still "keep my life together."

Eventually the relationship that I was in came to a close, and there was another wave of partying during that time in my life because again, I had made changes for someone else. The fact that I was "on top" again wasn't because I had turned back to the Lord. I didn't respect myself or my body.

A couple of years went by of "making it" at work. I had gotten a couple of promotions over these years, and on the outside, again, it appeared as though I had really overcome all of those dark times in my life. To everyone else, it looked like I had finally grown up. I still drank and dabbled in drugs, but I thought that was okay because overall I was doing fine.

God then put a man in my life. Notice that before I said I dated; this time, I know that this man was intentionally put in my life by God because there is no other explanation as to how or why he entered my life. It was as if God was tired of me not listening and was going to get my attention in a different way, through this man. I would say I have no idea why God kept blessing me or keeping me, but I do. It's the Lord keeping His promise that He will never leave nor forsake His children, even *though I kept taking and taking without giving, saying "thank you," or giving my life back to Him.*

For the first time someone helped me see value in myself and in my life. I started respecting myself, I quit drinking and doing drugs altogether, and I was actually very grounded for the first time, for me, and for no one else. This allowed me to see clearly for the first time in years, and I started to see how destructive I had truly been.

Because of this clarity, I started excelling at work. I was closer to my family than I had ever been. I really started to get back to my roots.

Over the course of ten years, I had one friend that never lost hope in me. We had gone to school together and knew each other since we were five. She never pushed the Bible on me or really brought up how I had been living my life. She mentioned that she had written a book about the story of Ruth, but I'm not a reader. I bought the book anyway, and somehow I sat there and read it cover to cover and the tears started flowing. It was time to come home to the Lord. I prayed and asked the Lord to capture my heart again. I repented and asked for forgiveness. I asked the Lord to take my earthly desires away and to give me strength.

God heard me, and He did exactly what I asked. Suddenly I had no desire to listen to mainstream music. I didn't want to watch TV. In fact, I sold both of my TVs. I started listening to only Christian music, and when a mainstream song would come on, I turned it off. I wanted nothing to do with anything that had not long ago encompassed every aspect of my life. My earthly desires were completely gone. I wanted nothing to do with anything that could cause me to slip once again.

God has blessed me in ways that I never even thought of. Even at work, in a secular workplace, I was given a mentor that "just so happened" to be a Christian that has become an accountability partner. But we know that nothing "just so happens" with God.

I have turned my life completely back to the Lord, and I have never felt closer to God or the people that I hurt for so long over the past ten years of my life. I have the desire to read my Bible and once again learn about the Lord as an adult. I look forward to serving the Lord for the rest of my life and I am forever thankful that God spared my life over and over again when I was ready to throw it away.

I share this story because if you are reading this, I want you to know that it is never too late to come back. No matter what you have done, no matter how far you have strayed, it is never, NEVER too late. Even if you're at a point in your life where you feel you've been lying to everyone about what you've done, it's always better to turn to God than to take the path that I did because you feel like you have already gone too far.

If you want to come home, God is waiting. If you are struggling with letting go of your habits and you ask for His help, He will extend his grace to you once again. There is no other true way to happiness, peace, and love.

Even though our actions have consequences, it is never too late to come back to God. I'm so thankful for His story of redemption in Christina's life and in my own life. It wasn't too late for Jonah to repent, but he chose to continue to run. He was about to find out the full extent of the consequences of his disobedience to God.

QUESTIONS FOR DISCUSSION

1. Has sin ever taken you farther than you wanted to go? Kept you longer than you wanted to stay? Cost you more than you wanted to pay?

2. Describe a time when God provided a "way of escape" for you to turn back to Him before it was too late.

3. What change can you make in your life now that will help you to avoid consequences later?

chapter four

THE HEART OF
THE MATTER

I ask God to search me
And know my deepest heart
Trusting I'll be free
To have a fresh start.

Jonah 1:4
But the Lord sent out a great wind into the sea,
and there was a mighty tempest in the sea, so that
the ship was like to be broken.

Jonah had made a choice to try to run from God,
and God was going to do whatever it took to get his
attention. He started with bringing a storm into
Jonah's life. It seemed that the ship that was bearing
the lives of Jonah and the crew was going to be broken.
The ship wasn't the only thing that was broken that

day; God was going to have to break Jonah to get his attention. When it seemed that the ship was going to go down, the crew began to take action.

> *Jonah 1:5*
> *Then the mariners were afraid, and cried every man unto his god, and cast forth the wares that were in the ship into the sea, to lighten it of them. But Jonah was gone down into the sides of the ship; and he lay, and was fast asleep.*

Things were going terribly wrong, so the sailors did the thing that seemed the most obvious: they started throwing things overboard to lighten the load of the ship. Meanwhile, Jonah, the true problem, was fast asleep in the depths of the ship.

How often do we try to do the same thing in our own lives? Things are starting to go south, and we have this feeling there's something that needs to change. So we start trying to clean up our lives. We throw overboard the things on the surface we think might be weighing us down. We try to overcome our addictions, we try to be kinder to the people around us. We think, "If I could just be a better person, I know things will shape up eventually." But things don't shape up. So we're forced to dig a little deeper.

> *Jonah 1:6*
> *So the shipmaster came to him, and said unto him,*

What meanest thou, O sleeper? arise, call upon thy God, if so be that God will think upon us, that we perish not.

The shipmaster remembered something, or rather, someone. He remembered Jonah, this not-so-secret stowaway. The sailors had called upon their gods in vain, so the shipmaster asked Jonah to give it a try. Perhaps the shipmaster had heard of this One True God that Jonah served; maybe He would be able to save them. He asked Jonah to help solve the problem, not realizing that Jonah was the problem. Perhaps Jonah prayed, but God did not answer. Jonah knew God wouldn't answer; God never answers the prayers of someone who is in direct rebellion to Him.

Psalm 66:18
If I regard iniquity in my heart, the Lord will not hear me:

Jonah's prayers seemingly fell on deaf ears, as did the prayers of the sailors. Somehow the sailors recognized that this was no ordinary storm. They would have been familiar with the weather patterns on this sea that they traversed so often. They knew that this storm was supernatural, and these heathen men discerned that the cause was some guilty party among them. They cast lots to determine who the guilty party was.

Jonah 1:7
And they said every one to his fellow, Come, and let us cast lots, that we may know for whose cause this evil is come upon us. So they cast lots, and the lot fell upon Jonah.

Jonah thought he had successfully hidden his disobedience, not only from the people around him, but also from God. Yet in the end, you can never truly hide your sin. One way or another, it will come to the light.

Numbers 32:23
...be sure your sin will find you out.

Jonah's sin had found him out, and it was time to get to the root of the problem before it was too late for everyone involved.

Jonah 1:8
Then said they unto him, Tell us, we pray thee, for whose cause this evil is upon us; What is thine occupation? and whence comest thou? what is thy country? and of what people art thou?

When we realize there is a problem in our lives that goes deeper than the surface symptoms, we must dig into it and get to its root if we are going to find a solution. The sailors had found that Jonah was the problem, so they asked probing questions of him. When I find that my deepest problem is myself, I have to ask some probing questions. This is rarely easy, and it's never fun. But until I do what it takes to get to the root of the problem, I'll never experience the positive life change I so desperately desire.

It's so much easier to stay in the dark, to believe that everything is just fine. I don't like to admit that there's a problem, and I especially don't like to admit when the problem is me. I like to think that I'm a pretty good person deep down. But I know that's not the case; in fact, the deeper I delve into my heart, I find that I'm rotten to the core.

Jeremiah 17:9
The heart is deceitful above all things, and desperately wicked: who can know it?

The truth is, your heart will lie to you. You can't trust it. It's wicked. Its nature is to sin. Who can know it? Not you. Not me. Only God can know our hearts.

Psalm 139:23-24
Search me, O God, and know my heart: try me, and know my thoughts: and see if there be any wicked way in me, and lead me in the way everlasting.

When I realize I have a problem, I have to ask probing questions, but it would be futile to ask the questions to myself. I can easily deceive myself into thinking that my intentions are good, that I'm doing fine. Only God can truly see the condition of my heart and the intentions of my thoughts. Asking God to search me and know my heart and thoughts can be terrifying. Why would I want the God of the universe to see if there's any wicked way in me? Because He is a God of mercy and compassion. When I ask Him to show me my wickedness, He does. And He shows me a better way, the way that leads to a fulfilling life in Him.

There's a lot of talk in our culture today about knowing yourself, getting to know who you truly are at your very core. Various personality assessments and online quizzes facilitate this trend of self-knowledge. I believe there's value in these to a certain extent, but they are far from a complete solution to the unrest in our souls. Yes, God created us with unique personalities, likes, and dislikes, and knowing what these are can be useful in our quest to serve Him with our skills. But the more I've tried to know myself, the more I come up short. Who I am at my very core is a sinner. When I spend time trying to get to know myself, I am not satisfied in the end.

What's truly fulfilling? Getting to know God. The more time I spend with God in His Word, the more I know Him. I understand His character, His personality, His likes, His dislikes. I see the purpose He has planned for everything under the sun. Just as He already knows who I am at my very core, every day I grow in my knowledge of who He is and the passions of His heart. I find far more fulfillment in making myself a student of God than making myself a student of me.

And you know what? The more I get to know God, the more I get to know myself as a result. I see how I fall short in light of His perfection. But I see how His grace has more than covered my deepest sin. I see His purpose for my life here on this earth. And I'm strengthened with the confidence that He made me exactly the way I am for a specific reason.

Right on par with knowing yourself is the popular concept of self care. Self care is defined as "the practice of taking an active role in protecting one's own well-being and happiness, in particular during periods of stress." The sad thing is, when we're focused on protecting our own happiness, we'll never find true joy. The Bible is clear that our calling is to imitate Jesus and put others before ourselves, just as He did.

Philippians 2:3-8
Let nothing be done through strife or vainglory; but in lowliness of mind let each esteem other better than themselves. Look not every man on his own things, but every man also on the things of others. Let this mind be in you, which was also in Christ Jesus: who, being in the form of God, thought it not robbery to be equal with God: but made himself of no reputation, and took upon him the form of a servant, and was made in the likeness of men:

and being found in fashion as a man, he humbled himself, and became obedient unto death, even the death of the cross.

Rather than being called to care for ourselves, Jesus calls us to deny ourselves. Yet it is in this losing of ourselves that we find true joy and purpose in life.

Mark 8:34-35
And when he had called the people unto him with his disciples also, he said unto them, Whosoever will come after me, let him deny himself, and take up his cross, and follow me. For whosoever will save his life shall lose it; but whosoever shall lose his life for my sake and the gospel's, the same shall save it.

Does this mean that we should never do anything for ourselves? Of course not. However, I believe we would be wise to use a filter of selflessness even when making the decision to do something for ourselves. Before doing something for myself, I try to ask these two questions:

- Am I neglecting the needs of others in order to do this thing for myself?
- Will the thing that I am about to do make me better equipped to serve others?

If I am not neglecting others, but am actually better equipping myself to be at my best to serve, doing something "for myself" can be completely unselfish.

I'm seeing a concept more and more frequently that is a rival to self care; it's soul care. My friend Kassie writes about this topic on her blog, "June and Joy." She defines soul care as, "Practicing habits which heal, strengthen, and grow your mind, personality, and emotional wellness." This goes so far beyond doing things to protect our happiness. This is simply doing what is necessary to care for our innermost being so that we can be at our best to serve others. In the same passage where Jesus tells us to deny ourselves, He tells us that we actually should care for our souls.

Mark 8:36-37
For what shall it profit a man, if he shall gain the whole world, and lose his own soul? Or what shall a man give in exchange for his soul?

God's desire for us to care for our souls starts with salvation, but it doesn't end there. Salvation is just the beginning of His good plan for our lives. He wants us to have a truly abundant life in the innermost part of ourselves, in our souls.

John 10:10
The thief cometh not, but for to steal, and to kill, and to destroy: I am come that they might have life, and that they might have it more abundantly.

God Himself cares for our souls, and He wants us

to do the same. In the book of Proverbs, Solomon admonishes us to do just that.

Proverbs 11:17
The merciful man doeth good to his own soul: but
he that is cruel troubleth his own flesh.

The word "soul" here is translated from the Hebrew word *nephesh,* meaning "the inner being of man." The phrase "doeth good" is translated from the Hebrew word *gamal,* meaning "to deal bountifully with." It's clear that God's desire is for us to care for our souls, but how do we actually do that? I have tried time and time again to care for my soul by finding identity and meaning in becoming the person God made me to be. I've searched the depths of my heart, and come up with different pieces of who I am that I think will give me fulfillment. I'm longing to find rest for my soul.

I've tried finding rest for my soul in a pursuit of physical fitness; I only came up empty.

I've tried finding rest for my soul in losing myself in good books; they never did satisfy.

I've tried finding rest for my soul in starting a family of my own; that has only proven to be more exhausting.

I've tried finding rest for my soul in writing; even that familiar outlet has left me unsatisfied.

None of these things are bad; in fact, they're all very good, and they're all regular and fulfilling parts of my life. They help me become the best version of myself so that I can serve others well. But they're not fulfilling at all when I'm trying to find total fulfillment in them. True rest for the soul can only be found in Jesus.

Matthew 11:28-30
Come unto me, all ye that labour and are heavy laden, and I will give you rest. Take my yoke upon you, and learn of me; for I am meek and lowly in heart: and ye shall find rest unto your souls. For my yoke is easy, and my burden is light.

Go to Him. He will give your soul rest. He will search and know your heart fully. And in being known of Him, you will more fully know yourself. It is then that you will be able to get to the heart of your troubles; only then will you be able to make the necessary adjustments to your life that will set you on the right course. Once you allow God to change you from the inside out, you will be more fully yourself than you ever have been before, set free to fulfill His beautiful purpose for your life.

The crew of the ship had asked Jonah all the right questions; it was time for him to give the answers that would lead to a solution for their perilous situation.

QUESTIONS FOR DISCUSSION

1. Has God ever had to break you to get your attention?

2. Have you ever tried to "clean up" your life on your own? What was the result?

3. Where have you tried to find rest for your soul, but you've come up short?

4. What do you need to do to find true rest for your soul?

5. What are some things you can do for yourself that are completely unselfish?

chapter five

ROWING HARDER

The try-hard life will never
Find success in the end.
To God my heart I tether
And on Him alone depend.

There was no use in hiding; Jonah was stuck in the middle of a stormy sea with these sailors, and he answered their questions in full.

Jonah 1:9
And he said unto them, I am an Hebrew; and I fear the Lord, the God of heaven, which hath made the sea and the dry land.

The word "fear" in this sense means, "to regard with reverence and awe." How true of a testimony was this? It didn't really seem to match up with his actions. Jonah was a hypocrite. And the crew of the ship knew it.

Jonah 1:10
Then were the men exceedingly afraid, and said unto him, Why hast thou done this? For the men knew that he fled from the presence of the Lord, because he had told them.

He had already told them that he was running from God's presence! Did he somehow think that was casual conversation? Apparently he hadn't told them that he was Jewish and that he "feared the Lord." Even though he was running from God, he knew that he was God's prophet. He knew his true identity, and he knew that his plan to run from God wasn't working. The crew of the ship could also see that his plan wasn't working, and they were quite concerned for their own lives.

Jonah 1:11
Then said they unto him, What shall we do unto thee, that the sea may be calm unto us? for the sea wrought, and was tempestuous.

Jonah knew the answer, and at last he was willing to put the welfare of others before his own.

Jonah 1:12
And he said unto them, Take me up, and cast me forth into the sea; so shall the sea be calm unto

*you: for I know that for my sake this great tempest
is upon you.*

Jonah knew that to save the ship, they would have
to get rid of the sin. And in this case, he was the sin.
He was the one who had displeased God. But the crew
did what we so often do when God convicts us of sin.

Jonah 1:13
*Nevertheless the men rowed hard to bring it to the
land; but they could not: for the sea wrought, and
was tempestuous against them.*

As I sit on the second floor of the coffee shop writing, I hear a tap on the window and see a shadow
mar the sunshine on the table on which my laptop is
perched. I look up to see a bee who has just flown into
the window, his first attempt at reaching the shade
and shelter of the cool indoors. There's another tap as
he makes his second attempt. Next, there are four taps
in close succession before he flies away, realizing his
trying was in vain.

How often are we like that bee? We think, *"If I just
tried harder, I could fix my situation."* So we try. Like
the sailors, we row harder. We fail again and again.
Because the problem isn't our lack of trying; the problem is our lack of giving up. If we want to get the victory, we have to give up. We have to give up our sin,
the thing that's holding us back. We have to realize

there is nothing we can do to save ourselves from the sin that condemns us. And until we do, we will be stuck in a perpetual state of working, rowing against waves that we cannot overcome. But hopefully, eventually we will come to the end of ourselves and cry out to the One who can save us.

Jonah 1:14-15
Wherefore they cried unto the Lord, and said, We beseech thee, O Lord, we beseech thee, let us not perish for this man's life, and lay not upon us innocent blood: for thou, O Lord, hast done as it pleased thee. So they took up Jonah, and cast him forth into the sea: and the sea ceased from her raging.

They called upon the Lord to save them, just as you and I must do.

Romans 10:9-10, 13
That if thou shalt confess with thy mouth the Lord Jesus, and shalt believe in thine heart that God hath raised him from the dead, thou shalt be saved. For with the heart man believeth unto righteousness; and with the mouth confession is made unto salvation...for whosoever shall call upon the name of the Lord shall be saved.

That's all God asks of us. Just believe. Just trust Him. We repent of our sin, cast it overboard, and we are forgiven. But often the natural thing that follows is what happened in the case of Jonah and the ship's crew.

Jonah 1:16
Then the men feared the Lord exceedingly, and offered a sacrifice unto the Lord, and made vows.

To trust God is enough, as salvation is by grace. But it's only natural that when we call out to God to save us, our lives change as well.

2 Corinthians 5:17
Therefore if any man be in Christ, he is a new creature: old things are passed away; behold, all things are become new.

A change in our lifestyle is not a requirement for salvation, but rather a result of salvation. However, some new believers long to hang on to the sin that once separated them from God. But as long as they do, it will not go well with them. The sea of their life will continue to rage. We must come to the place where we are in agreement with God about our sin, both in word and in deed.

Galatians 5:1
Stand fast therefore in the liberty wherewith Christ hath made us free, and be not entangled again with the yoke of bondage.

Christian liberty is a touchy topic; does it mean

that now that we're believers we can do whatever we want? Absolutely not! Christ didn't make us free so we could do whatever we want; He made us free from the bondage of our sin. Yet many believers fall into the trap of believing they can keep living a lifestyle that displeases God because He will forgive them.

Romans 6:1-2
What shall we say then? Shall we continue in sin, that grace may abound? God forbid. How shall we, that are dead to sin, live any longer therein?

Our old nature is dead; we have no reason to keep going back to it. We're fooling ourselves if we think freedom is found in continuing in sin. True freedom is found in submission to Christ. The same One who gives us rest for our souls offers for us to trade the burdensome yoke of sin for one much lighter.

Matthew 11:28-30
Come unto me, all ye that labour and are heavy laden, and I will give you rest. Take my yoke upon you, and learn of me; for I am meek and lowly in heart: and ye shall find rest unto your souls. For my yoke is easy, and my burden is light.

What a beautiful picture of what Christ longs to do for us as believers. We don't have to try harder to live a life that is pleasing to Him any more than we have to try harder to solve our sin problem. We just have to allow Him to come alongside us and share the burden. The picture here is of oxen pulling a load. Imagine one ox pulling a load far greater than he can bear. Then another ox is brought alongside him; a wooden yoke is put over their necks, and they begin to pull the load together. The two oxen are then able to pull a load more than twice as heavy as one of them could have pulled alone. The burden of living a set apart life doesn't have to fall on us alone; Jesus longs to be on the other side of the yoke. And I'm certain that He is able to carry more than His fair share of the burden. He will teach us, and we can finally have rest from a life lived in our own strength.

I have been a small person my entire life. Nevertheless, I'm usually undeterred by feats of strength. In fact, a feeling of a need to prove myself has often pushed me to do a little more than I should have attempted. When I think of the futility of my own strength, I'm reminded of a story from the first year of my marriage.

Being poor newlyweds, we didn't have much money for furniture. When we moved into the basement apartment of a family in our church, we were thankful that they allowed us to borrow some living room furniture. However, most of that living room furniture was actually their patio furniture. We moved in in January, and we were happy to provide winter storage for their patio furniture. That meant we could put off buying living room furniture! But even in Utah, the weather warmed up eventually, and our gracious landlords were ready to move their patio furniture to the patio where it belonged.

They came in one evening after dinner, and Steven helped them move the furniture from our living room to the patio. The tiny leather sofa (which also belonged to our landlords) remaining in the middle of the room was a sad sight to behold. And the look in my eyes mirrored that sad sight. Steven encouraged me that this was our opportunity to acquire some living room furniture of our own. So, I searched the local classified ads with vigor and found the perfect piece to fill the void in our newly emptied living room.

It was a coffee table. Not just any coffee table; the *perfect* coffee table. It was made of a solid tree stump, and it was gorgeous. And we would only have to drive an hour one way to pick it up! We contacted the seller to ask for exact measurements. I mean, we had to make sure this monstrosity of a tree stump would fit into the trunk of our two door Honda Civic. We determined it would work, and being the young, energetic people that we were, we got up early one morning to go pick it up before Steven went to work.

Loading it into the trunk of the car went off without a hitch. The man selling it helped my husband carry it to the car, and it fit into the trunk as if the little Honda was made for such a time as this. We made the drive back home, the proud owners of the most beautiful coffee table in the world. The problem arose when we got home. There was no one to help Steven carry the table around the back of the house and down the stairs to our basement apartment. No one, that is, except me.

I was in the best physical shape of my life at this point, but I recognized immediately that I would not be able to be any help whatsoever. The table likely weighed two-hundred pounds, which wouldn't have deterred me if I thought there was a place I could easily grip. But my arms were too short to encompass the massive chunk of a tree, and I despaired at the thought of trying.

Steven, undeterred, didn't want to wait for someone else to help him bring the coffee table into the house. So it would have to be me. Heart racing and hands clammy (which didn't help the situation), I made my best effort. Steven wrapped his arms around the stump, and I grappled to find a hand hold. We walked like that for a few feet. And this is what I imagine being in the yoke with Jesus must be like. I knew that I wasn't doing anything to help move that table. My arms were touching it, and I was giving my best effort. I had some scrapes and bruises on my arms for a few weeks to prove that I had tried. But Steven was doing one hundred percent of the work that day.

The reality is, after a few steps, I gave up. I admitted

that I couldn't carry the burden, or even help. And somehow, Steven got it into our living room without breaking his back.

How much more peace would we have in our lives if we let go of the burden of living a good enough life to please God and let Jesus carry the load? After all, if we've accepted His gift of salvation, we are already good enough in God's eyes. When God sees us, He sees the righteousness of Jesus.

2 Corinthians 5:21
For he hath made him to be sin for us, who knew
no sin; that we might be made the righteousness of
God in him.

When the crew threw Jonah, the sin problem, into the sea, the sea was instantly calm. Even in Jonah's disobedience, God was able to use him to show Himself to these unbelievers. They saw the awe and power of God, and their lives were changed.

Perhaps the sailors were Jonah's first converts in our story. When Jonah put the needs of others before his own, sacrificing himself for the safety of the sailors, God was able to use him for His glory. What a gracious God to use Jonah, the prophet who was trying to hide from His presence, to get the attention of these men He loved. But at the same time, God was still trying to get the attention of Jonah, and it was going to take more than a storm to get the job done.

QUESTIONS FOR DISCUSSION

1. What aspect of your life are you trying hard to fix?

2. Are you carrying a weight that is too heavy for you? What is it?

3. What would it look like for you to allow Jesus to carry your load for you?

chapter six

TO WHOM MUCH
IS GIVEN

I will steward faithfully
The truth I've received.
Meeting God daily,
His promises I'll believe.

We've come to a point in the book of Jonah that most
children who have grown up in church are familiar
with. But the story of Jonah and the whale is much
more than a fun children's story.

Jonah 1:17
Now the Lord had prepared a great fish to swal-
low up Jonah. And Jonah was in the belly of the fish
three days and three nights.

Jonah had been cast overboard, but God had not

forsaken him. God prepared a "great fish" to swallow him and prevent him from drowning. But what was the "great fish?" We don't really know. The Hebrew words used here literally mean "big fish." The Bible does not tell us what kind of fish it was; it could have been anything. So why do we say that it was a whale? This common interpretation actually does come from the Bible.

> *Matthew 12:40*
> *For as Jonas was three days and three nights in the whale's belly; so shall the Son of man be three days and three nights in the heart of the earth.*

In our English New Testament, Jesus refers to the fish that swallowed Jonah as a whale. But the New Testament wasn't written in English; it was written in Greek. The Greek word that is translated as "whale" here also means large fish, or even sea monster. It's likely that the translators chose the word "whale" because that was the largest fish they could imagine. But perhaps in the days of Jesus, the people listening to Him would have understood this term completely differently. Sea monsters such as the leviathan are mentioned in the Bible in such a way that implies the original reader would have understood what this was. Maybe Jonah was swallowed by some kind of sea monster that doesn't even exist anymore, or maybe there's still one out there lurking in the depths of the sea.

However, this is all conjecture. The truth of the matter is, it doesn't matter what kind of fish swallowed Jonah. What matters is the way God used this miraculous occurrence in the life of Jonah and as a message to His people in generations to come. Even though Jonah had been disobedient, God was using his life once more. If we look at the full context of what Jesus was saying in this passage in Matthew, we see that, in part, God allowed Jonah to be swallowed by the fish in order to use him as an example.

Matthew 12:39-41
But he answered and said unto them, An evil and adulterous generation seeketh after a sign; and there shall no sign be given to it, but the sign of the prophet Jonas: for as Jonas was three days and three nights in the whale's belly; so shall the Son of man be three days and three nights in the heart of the earth. The men of Nineveh shall rise in judgment with this generation, and shall condemn it: because they repented at the preaching of Jonas; and, behold, a greater than Jonas is here.

Jonah's time in the belly of the fish for three days and three nights was a picture of Jesus, who would die and be buried for three days and three nights before rising again. Jesus used Jonah as an illustration in his preaching, stating that the men of Nineveh would be found righteous at the judgment day, but those to whom Jesus was speaking would be condemned. Why? Because (spoiler alert) the people of Nineveh chose to repent, but the people who were hearing Jesus, who was God Himself, did not repent.

What about you? You've never had a prophet come to you with a special message from God, and you've never seen Jesus in the flesh. But you have something that generations of people have not had: access to the complete Word of God in your own language. Sadly, many people today still don't have the privilege of reading God's Word in their own language. But if you're reading this book, you do. You have access to God's inspired truth in written form. What have you done with it? Have you even read it all the way through one time? Do you even know what the Lord requires of you?

Luke 12:48
...For unto whomsoever much is given, of him shall be much required:...

God has given you all the access to truth that you need through His Word. You have been given much. The prophet Micah summed up what God requires of us very well:

Micah 6:8
He hath shewed thee, O man, what is good; and what doth the Lord require of thee, but to do

*justly, and to love mercy, and to walk humbly
with thy God?*

Do justly.

Love mercy.

Walk humbly with your God.

It all sounds so simple, but how do we know what
is just? How do we know what is merciful? How do
we walk with God? All of this can be accomplished
through a daily time in God's Word. When we are daily
walking with God, He will show us what is good and
just, and we will be able to live the life He desires us to
live. We will be held accountable for how we respond
to the revelation of truth that has been given to us.
Will God find that we have been good stewards?

My daily time with God is the most essential part
of my day. I don't just say this because it sounds good;
I say it because I've learned through experience that
the more of God's truth I absorb every day, the better
equipped I am to be the person He wants me to be.
And I've come to realize that when I'm being the person God wants me to be, I feel the most alive and the
most like myself.

I have to be honest here: sticking to routines comes
pretty easily for me. I spent years before I had even accepted Christ reading the Bible every single day. But
it wasn't because I was hungry for God's truth; it was
because I wanted to check Bible reading off my to-do
list and be able to say I read the Bible every day that

week. After I trusted Christ, my perspective slowly changed, and I started reading with the intention of getting to know God better. It wasn't an overnight change, but more and more my motivation is a desperate need to know God and experience His hope in my everyday life.

Our world has an epidemic of emptiness. I believe we feel that emptiness acutely in America because we have so many opportunities to try to fill it. We live in a land of plenty. Our souls are longing to be filled, so we try to fill the void with countless comforts.

Shopping.

Good food.

Entertainment.

Relationships.

None of these things are wrong in and of themselves, but when we try to fill the void in our souls with these things, we only feel emptier. The problem is, we're trying to fill our souls with spiritual junk food rather than finding our satisfaction in God. When I left my house today, my toddler was having the time of her life snacking on a soft pretzel. I loved seeing how much happiness that soft pretzel brought to her. But if I only gave her soft pretzels for breakfast, lunch, and dinner for the rest of the month, she would soon start to feel some negative effects. A soft pretzel is a fun snack, but it's not going to satisfy my daughter's need for nutrition. Tonight we'll make sure she has a nutrient rich dinner that will meet her needs and contribute to normal growth.

Unfortunately, I don't really have anyone monitoring my spiritual diet for me. It's easy to consume more than my fair share of spiritual junk food in an attempt to satisfy my soul. I most often indulge in spiritual junk food on my phone. I reach for my phone in moments of quiet when I feel the anxiety creeping in. What if I instead reached out to God in prayer? There's nothing wrong with enjoying the good things God has given to me in this life, even the good things that can be found on my phone. But if I'm trying to satisfy the longings of my soul with those things, I'm always going to end up empty. If I want to be filled, I have to change what I'm hungry for.

Matthew 5:6
Blessed are they which do hunger and thirst after righteousness: for they shall be filled.

What are you hungry for? Is it the righteousness of God found in His Word? Or is it something else? Sometimes changing our appetites simply starts with feeding ourselves with the right things and trusting the process. I know when I exercise and eat nutritious foods, I feel good. But somehow it's easy to forget that when I get into the habit of lounging on the couch with a Pop-Tart and a good book. Sometimes I just have to get up and do what I know is right, even if I don't feel like it. When I start to feel the good results of my daily choice to skip the Pop-Tarts and go to the gym, I start to actually have a hunger for exercise and vegetables. This doesn't mean I never eat Pop-Tarts; it just means that they're in their proper place in my life.

Spending time in God's Word is much the same. It's easy to forget just what a difference time with the Lord can make in our lives when we get into the habit of filling our time with other things. Sometimes we just have to do what we know is right, even if we don't feel like it. It may not sound very spiritual, but it's just plain faithfulness. Eventually, we begin to experience the positive results of a daily time with God, and we're encouraged to keep going. Obviously we don't need to read God's Word every moment of every day; our lives will include many other activities. But when we're truly hungry for God's Word, those activities will stay in their proper place in our lives.

Even as Jonah unknowingly preached a sermon about following Jesus to us with his life, he was held accountable for the truth he knew about God as well. And the time had come for him to turn to the One who had been trying to get his attention all along.

QUESTIONS FOR DISCUSSION

1. Have you been a good steward of the truth God has revealed to you through His Word? Do you know what the Bible says?

2. What spiritual junk food do you struggle with trying to find satisfaction in?

3. What can you do today to create a routine of filling yourself with the satisfying truth of God's Word?

chapter seven

DESPERATE TIMES CALL FOR DESPERATE PRAYERS

Desperately I pray,
For desperate is my need.
I know no other way,
So for God's grace I plead.

Jonah opened his eyes, and he was pleasantly surprised that he hadn't drowned. But he may have soon wondered if his fate was worse: he found himself in the belly of a fish.

My husband is trying to convert me to being a fish eater. In fact, I wouldn't be surprised if I went home tonight and found that fish was on the menu for dinner, as it has been his custom recently to have fish on the table when I come home from my writing day on Fridays. Overall, I would say it's going well. I've successfully eaten fish for several meals. But I haven't historically had an affinity for fish in any way, shape, or form.

The taste of most fish disgusts me, as does the smell of *all* fish. I don't know who first caught a fish and decided, in spite of its rotten smell, to eat it. I almost hesitate to say I've ever been fishing because I've never baited my own hook, nor have I touched the fish I reeled in. The feeling of scales gives me a nails-on-a-chalkboard kind of feeling. Our local aquarium has an exhibit in which you can touch the fish. I believe I did so in a young, formative year of my life, and my instincts quickly told me that I most decidedly did *not* want to touch a fish ever again. This is why we've never had an aquarium in our home. My family kept fish as pets when I was young, but I never had to clean the tank. My dad took care of the disgusting task, and I'm pretty sure he intentionally touched the fish when he did. I clearly don't understand the thought process behind this.

Although I love going to aquariums to a certain extent, there's always a little anxiety involved at some point during an aquarium visit for me. The majestic giants of the oceans and rivers are awe inspiring. But, I mean, what if the glass suddenly shattered? All that disgusting fish water would just wash over us, and we would be surrounded by the scaly monsters, doomed to die from that nails-on-a-chalkboard sensation. This also explains why I don't swim in lakes or the ocean.

Jonah quickly went from being in my worst nightmare, surrounded by scales, to being in a situation far worse than my worst nightmare. If fish smell that bad on the outside, how bad did that fish smell from the inside? I would guess his first reaction would be to vomit. And then the smell of human vomit is added to the smell of fish guts and everything else the fish ate that day. Which was likely other fish. Talk about the lowest of the low. I don't know if Jonah vomited or not, but I do know that his reaction was to pray.

The prayers that we read were certainly the true thoughts of Jonah's heart, but I doubt they were actually the words he prayed in that desperate situation. The words we read are composed and put together; many of them echo the Psalms that the prophet would have been familiar with. It's likely that when he was writing this account after the fact, he wrote down the truth of what he experienced in his prayer in a poetic way, true to the style of the time. But I believe the prayer that he must have prayed in his initial moments in the whale's belly would have been a little more desperate sounding. Based on one of my own personal experiences, I know that desperate times call for desperate prayers.

In the summer before my senior year of college, I was driving to work, just as I did every day. It was a normal drive to work – until an SUV started coming into my lane. I was in the far left lane, so there was nowhere for me to go. I swerved into the little space between my lane and the retaining wall and honked my horn. The SUV got back in its lane, but when I tried to get back in my lane, something went wrong. My car started spinning. I was completely disoriented, trying desperately to turn my wheel and figure out where I even was. When my car seemed to right itself, I didn't see what I wanted to see; instead, I saw four lanes of oncoming traffic. I was terrified. I turned the wheel to try to get my car going in the right direction, but I just kept spinning. I was quite disoriented, but I believe I spun a total of two times as I made my way across the interstate before I crashed into the retaining wall on the far right. My car finally came to a stop, and I climbed out through the passenger side. I was just thankful to be alive.

In the days and months following my wreck, the events of that day replayed over and over in my mind. I remembered the sight of interstate traffic coming toward me. I remembered the sight of the retaining wall rushing to the side of my car and then making contact. I remembered the sensation of my head hitting the side window and the sting that lingered in the days following. But the things I remembered the most weren't the sights or the sensations; the things I remembered the most were the sounds. I remembered the sound of my scream, a helpless, unheard scream, piercing the air when I realized my car was facing the wrong way, when I thought I was going to die. I remembered the sound of the metal of my car smashing into the concrete wall, followed by the sound of my head hitting the window. But the sound I remembered the most was the one that rang out between my scream and the car hitting the wall. That was the sound of my prayer. After I screamed, when I thought my life was coming to an end, I cried out to God in a way I had never done before. My prayer was not pretty or composed. Rather, it came out of the desperation of my heart. I simply cried out, "God, please save me! God, please save me!"

When we find ourselves faced with death, we learn to pray in a more desperate way than we have ever prayed before. There's another man in the Bible who was faced with the prospect of drowning, just as Jonah was. His prayer that was recorded is a little more along the lines of what I believe Jonah must have prayed in those initial moments in the whale's belly. In Matthew 14, the account is given of Peter walking on water. He had the faith to step out of the boat, but when he looked away from the Lord, he began to sink.

Matthew 14:30
But when he saw the wind boisterous, he was afraid; and beginning to sink, he cried, saying, Lord, save me.

When we read that verse, we tend to read it calmly, as if Peter is speaking calmly. But I believe that Peter was shouting in terror. Because he probably was! He thought he was going to drown! He saw the circumstances, and he cried out in desperation. Although Jonah's initial desperate prayer isn't recorded for us, we can learn much from the thoughts of his heart in the belly of the whale that have been preserved for us all these years later.

Jonah 2:1-2
Then Jonah prayed unto the Lord his God out of the fish's belly, and said, I cried by reason of mine affliction unto the Lord, and he heard me; out of the belly of hell cried I, and thou heardest my voice.

Jonah knew that even in his misery, even in the worst situation he had ever been in, God had not forgotten him. He knew God heard him. And he knew God had taken care of him. I mean, Jonah really deserved to drown. But somehow he was still alive. Even in this desperate situation, he was able to see God's grace. But he also saw God's judgment.

Jonah 2:3
For thou hadst cast me into the deep, in the midst of the seas; and the floods compassed me about: all thy billows and thy waves passed over me.

Jonah knew that God was chastening him because

of his disobedience. He knew he would not have been in this situation if he had just obeyed God and gone to Nineveh when he was told. Yet here he was, in the depths of the sea, in the belly of the whale. Even in this desperate situation, he acknowledges that the billows and waves were ordained of God. God had a purpose, even in this.

Jonah 2:4
Then I said, I am cast out of thy sight; yet will I look again toward thy holy temple.

Funny enough, Jonah thought that now he really *was* in a place where God couldn't see him. He said he was in "the belly of hell." The Hebrew word translated as "hell" here could be translated as "the grave." Jonah figured this was the end. This would be the place where he would die, and he was probably too far away for God to see him. But I'm once again reminded of the truth of Psalm 139.

Psalm 139:7-10
Whither shall I go from thy spirit? or whither shall I flee from thy presence? If I ascend up into heaven, thou art there: if I make my bed in hell, behold, thou art there. If I take the wings of the morning, and dwell in the uttermost parts of the sea; even there shall thy hand lead me, and thy right hand shall hold me.

Jonah had not gone too far for God to see him, nor could he ever be beyond God's sight and God's care. Even though he thought God could no longer see him, he did the only thing he knew to do: he looked toward God's holy temple. This is in reference to Solomon's prayer upon the completion of the temple.

2 Chronicles 6:36-39
If they sin against thee, (for there is no man which sinneth not,) and thou be angry with them, and deliver them over before their enemies, and they carry them away captives unto a land far off or near; yet if they bethink themselves in the land whither they are carried captive, and turn and pray unto thee in the land of their captivity, saying, We have sinned, we have done amiss, and have dealt wickedly; if they return to thee with all their heart and with all their soul in the land of their captivity, whither they have carried them captives, and pray toward their land, which thou gavest unto their fathers, and toward the city which thou hast chosen, and toward the house which I have built for thy name: then hear thou from the heavens, even from thy dwelling place, their prayer and their supplications, and maintain their cause, and forgive thy people which have sinned against thee.

Perhaps Jonah wondered if being carried into captivity included being trapped in the belly of a fish. He certainly knew that the reason for his own captivity was his sin against God, and he knew that God was the One who had delivered him into his stinky prison. It was certainly no coincidence that he found himself alive in the belly of a whale! Of course he didn't know which direction the temple would have been, as he was completely disoriented in his underwater abode. But it was not his eyes that he was turning toward the temple; it was his heart.

Why were the Israelites to look toward the temple? We worship a living God, not a place! But before the resurrection of Christ, God the Holy Spirit did not dwell within His people; He dwelled in the temple. Jonah was turning his heart toward the physical dwelling place of God, and in turn, he was turning his heart toward God.

Jonah 2:5
The waters compassed me about, even to the soul: the depth closed me round about, the weeds were wrapped about my head.

Jonah describes his physical state. First the water of the ocean surrounded him, and then the combination of water and stomach acid in the belly of the whale. He felt the immensity of it all in the innermost part of his being. The Hebrew word used for "weeds" here simply means "a water plant." Seaweed. He had seaweed wrapped around his head. The feeling of seaweed wrapped around my feet as I wade into the ocean is enough to make me never want to wade more than ankle deep, but here we find Jonah literally in the weeds. He was at his wit's end.

Jonah 2:6-7
I went down to the bottoms of the mountains; the earth with her bars was about me for ever: yet hast thou brought up my life from corruption, O LORD my God. When my soul fainted within me I re-membered the LORD: and my prayer came in unto thee, into thine holy temple.

Jonah realized he had sunk as low as he possibly could go, quite literally. He had reached the end of his strength, but he knew that there was One whose strength was far greater. So he prayed. This prophet who had run from God knew in the deepest place of his heart that God had not forgotten him. He knew that God heard his prayer, no matter what direction the temple was. God heard his cry from the belly of the whale.

Jonah 2:8
They that observe lying vanities forsake their own mercy.

Here Jonah acknowledges that it was no use trying to fool himself. He had succumbed to a false narrative of who God was. His actions said that he believed God to be someone he could simply hide from, ignoring the commands that he wasn't fond of. In reality, his disobedience was a form of idolatry. He valued his own comfort and safety more than he valued his commitment to God. But he knew the truth: the one he was harming most by disobeying God was himself.

Jonah 2:9
But I will sacrifice unto thee with the voice of thanksgiving; I will pay that that I have vowed. Salvation is of the LORD.

When we think of thankfulness, perhaps we think of thanking God for the abundance of good things in our lives. But God commands us to be thankful not just for the pleasant things, but in all things.

Ephesians 5:20
Giving thanks always for all things unto God and the Father in the name of our Lord Jesus Christ;

1 Thessalonians 5:18
In every thing give thanks: for this is the will of God in Christ Jesus concerning you.

When I am in the depths, thanksgiving feels like a sacrifice. Jonah knew this as well, and he acknowledged just how much of a sacrifice thanksgiving was for him in that moment. But he gave thanks to God anyway, and he rededicated himself to doing the work that he had committed himself to in the first place. He was God's prophet, and he was ready to declare God's message.

Finally in his prayer Jonah acknowledged that God had saved him from certain death. You would think that he now understood that God's love was directed towards His wayward prophet just as much as it was directed toward the wicked people of Nineveh. But as we'll soon see, this wasn't the case.

QUESTIONS FOR DISCUSSION

1. Has there been a time in your life where you have prayed to God out of desperation? Describe that prayer.

2. How would your prayer life change if you always prayed with such passion?

3. Is it hard for you to praise God when you are "in the depths?" Why or why not?

chapter eight

SECOND CHANCES

A chance at living
Undeserved.
My all I'm giving
To others serve.

God heard Jonah's prayer, and He answered.

Jonah 2:10
And the Lord spake unto the fish, and it vomited
out Jonah upon the dry land.

Jonah soon finds himself on the shore in a pile of fish vomit. I'm not quite sure what answer he had in mind; maybe he thought God could supernaturally transport him from the belly of the fish to dry land and clean him up a little bit. God could have chosen to do that, but He chose to use more natural means.

And when you think about the natural alternative, fish vomit doesn't seem that bad. God loved this messy prophet on the shore so much that even in his filth, He spoke to him once more.

> *Jonah 3:1-2*
> *And the word of the Lord came unto Jonah the second time, saying, arise, go unto Nineveh, that great city, and preach unto it the preaching that I bid thee.*

God's command had not changed, but the recipient of his command was a changed man. So He speaks to Jonah once more and gives him a second chance. Jonah received a second chance in two ways: the first was physically. Jonah should have drowned in the ocean, or at least found his death in the belly of the whale, but God gave him a second chance at life. When someone has been given a second chance at life, they often begin to live quite differently.

In the fall of 2016, my dad was involved in a chemical explosion at the factory where he worked. He suffered from chemical burns over 40% of his body, traumatic amputation of two fingers, and many broken bones. But the most severe of his injuries was chemical inhalation; his lungs were not able to function on their own. That night in the intensive care burn unit, a very skilled and intelligent doctor met with us in a side room. The lights were dim, and the circumstances were even darker. She painted a very grim picture for us; if something didn't change for the better over the course of the night, my dad would not survive.

But we prayed, and God answered. My dad did survive, and he healed far more quickly and far more completely than any doctor predicted. The Great Physician took complete control and gave my dad miraculous healing. God gave my dad a second chance at life, and I have had the privilege of observing the many ways he has not taken that second chance for granted.

Even in his early days in the rehab facility when he was able to talk again, I watched as he witnessed to nurses in a more bold way than I knew was natural for his introverted personality. I've watched as he has invested in his relationships more urgently, knowing that life can be taken at any moment. I've watched as he's taken better care of his health, realizing that the ability to do so is a gift from God. Even just watching how much more thoroughly he enjoys the little pleasures of life, like a big bowl of ice cream, has brought joy to my heart.

God *is* the God of second chances.

Not only did God give Jonah a second chance at life physically, but He also gave him a second chance spiritually to live for Him. God has given this type of second chance to those who didn't deserve it since the beginning of time.

When Adam and Eve ate of the fruit in the garden,

they earned for themselves the penalty of death. But God set in motion His plan for the redemption of all mankind, not only giving Adam and Eve a second chance, but also giving a second chance to you and me. We've all been given this opportunity at a second chance, but have we taken it?

Jesus came to die so that we might have life. If we have accepted His gift of salvation, we have been given a second chance far greater than we ever deserved. But what have we done with that second chance? Has anything changed? Or have we stayed the same as we were before? God's desire is that the second chance He has given us would bring about a life change.

2 Corinthians 5:17
Therefore if any man be in Christ, he is a new creature: old things are passed away; behold, all things are become new.

What are we doing with the second chance God has given us? Are we being bold witnesses for Him? Are we cultivating relationships with people, knowing that those souls are the only thing that will last for eternity? Are we taking care of our spiritual health, seeking God daily, getting to know Him better and better? Perhaps one of the best things we can do with the second chance God has given us is to give second chances to others. In the New Testament, Peter asks Jesus a memorable question about giving second chances.

Matthew 18:21-22

Then came Peter to him, and said, Lord how oft shall my brother sin against me, and I forgive him? till seven times? Jesus saith unto him, I say not unto thee, Until seven times: but, Until seventy times seven.

Peter thought it was reasonable to give a second chance, even to give a seventh chance! But Jesus tells us that we should be willing to give a four-hundred-ninetieth chance. After all, God has likely given us far more than that many chances. Jesus further illustrates his point with a parable, one of his masterful stories.

Matthew 18:23-25

Therefore is the kingdom of heaven likened unto a certain king, which would take account of his servants. And when he had begun to reckon, one was brought unto him, which owed him ten thousand talents. But forasmuch as he had not to pay, his lord commanded him to be sold, and his wife, and children, and all that he had, and payment to be made.

The king in this story represents God, and the servant is us. This servant owed the king a great debt which he never would have been able to repay. The king assigned a punishment that was completely deserved: if the servant could not repay his debt, he would be forced to repay with his life and the lives of those in his household. But the servant begged for mercy.

Matthew 18:26-27
The servant therefore fell down, and worshipped him, saying, Lord, have patience with me, and I will pay thee all. Then the Lord of that servant was moved with compassion, and loosed him, and forgave him the debt.

The king, representing God, forgave the servant of his debt and erased all the consequences associated with it. Can you imagine how overjoyed this servant was? He had been given a second chance at life. Surely his life would look different from then on! The next part of the story sadly tells us this wasn't the case.

Matthew 18:28-29
But the same servant went out, and found one of his fellowservants, which owed him an hundred pence: and he laid hands on him, and took him by the throat, saying, Pay me that thou owest. And his fellowservant fell down at his feet, and besought him, saying, Have patience with me, and I will pay thee all.

Another servant of the king owed a debt to this man. It was a small one, and honestly he could have paid it if he were given the time. The first servant was harsh to this servant initially, but surely he would have mercy when his fellow servant begged for more time. He wasn't asking for the debt to be forgiven; he was willing to pay in full. He just needed a little more time.

Matthew 18:30
And he would not: but went and cast him into prison, till he should pay the debt.

He refused. He pressed charges against the servant and had him thrown into prison. I don't know what hope he had that the man would be able to repay the debt while he was in prison, but in his anger, he didn't care. This man owed him money, and if he didn't pay right now there would be consequences. He had seemingly forgotten the great forgiveness that had been granted to him.

Matthew 18:31-33
So when his fellowservants saw what was done, they were very sorry, and came and told unto their lord all that was done. Then his lord, after that he had called him, said unto him, O thou wicked servant, I forgave thee all that debt, because thou desiredst me: shouldest not thou also have had compassion on thy fellowservant, even as I had pity on thee?

The king rebuked him, but we are the ones who are

really rebuked. God has forgiven us so much, giving us a second chance at life that we didn't deserve. He forgave a debt that we never could have paid. But how often do we refuse to show compassion on those who have done us wrong? How often do we measure out the judgment that others deserve rather than forgiving them undeservedly as God has forgiven us?

If we're not making the most out of the second chance God has given us, it's time to get up and do what we know God has called us to do.

Jonah 3:3a
So Jonah arose, and went unto Nineveh, according to the word of the Lord.

God said go, and Jonah went. His actions were finally right, but his motivation may not have been what God intended for it to be. He had accepted God's second chance in his own life, but he couldn't have cared less if the Ninevites accepted a second chance or not. The wayward prophet still had some lessons to learn.

QUESTIONS FOR DISCUSSION

1. Have you or someone you know been given a second chance at life physically? How is that person's life different as a result of that second chance?

2. Have you accepted Christ as your Savior, receiving the spiritual second chance He gives you at life? If so, what have you done with that second chance?

3. If you have not used your second chance at life well, what could you do to change that today?

chapter nine

THE INFLUENCE OF ONE

A difference I'll make
To all in my path
As a stand I do take
For God's truth that lasts.

Jonah 3:3b-4
Now Nineveh was an exceeding great city of three
days' journey. And Jonah began to enter into the
city a day's journey, and he cried, and said, Yet for-
ty days, and Nineveh shall be overthrown.

Preaching the message of repentance to Nineveh
was no small task; there wasn't a First Baptist Church
of Nineveh in which Jonah could preach his message.
It would take him three days to travel across the whole
city, preaching as he went. But in obedience to God,
he started out. I doubt he expected much to happen.

At best, these wicked people would ignore the crazy preacher, and he would do his duty and go on his way. At worst, they would kill him. However, on the first day's journey, Jonah witnessed an unexpected miracle.

Jonah 3:5
So the people of Nineveh believed God, and proclaimed a fast, and put on sackcloth, from the greatest of them even to the least of them.

The people were repenting! They were turning from their wicked ways and turning to the one true God! Why the sudden change? Perhaps the catalyst for the repentance was more surprising than the repentance itself.

Jonah 3:6
For word came unto the king of Nineveh, and he arose from his throne, and he laid his robe from him, and covered him with sackcloth, and sat in ashes.

The king himself, the most influential person in all of Nineveh, heard the message that Jonah was preaching, and God convicted his heart of his sin, as only God could have done. This was a man who had been complacent. He had the power to affect change in his nation, but he had grown comfortable with the wickedness around him. But God is able to soften even the hardest of hearts, and the king turned to Him.

Jonah 3:7-8

And he caused it to be proclaimed and published through Nineveh by the decree of the king and his nobles, saying, Let neither man nor beast, herd nor flock, taste any thing: let them not feed, nor drink water: but let man and beast be covered with sackcloth, and cry mightily unto God: yea, let them turn every one from his evil way, and from the violence that is in their hands.

He chose to use his influence for good by calling everyone under his authority to turn to God as well. This does raise a question: Were those conversions genuine? Maybe some of them weren't. Maybe some of them were simply trying to stay on the good side of the king. But God looks on the heart. He knew which conversions were genuine, and He was ready to show mercy.

There is something to be learned from the example of the king of Nineveh. I'm not saying that you should command everyone you may have authority over to turn to the Lord. When we pressure others to believe in Jesus, we do risk the possibility of false professions of faith. I don't ever want to be responsible for giving someone a false sense of security. Even so, we can learn from the king of Nineveh to be intentional about using our influence for good.

"But I don't have an influence. I'm not anybody important."

Oh, but you do have an influence. And you are important. You may not have an influence over a nation, but you don't need to be famous to have an influence. God has put people in your life who are looking to you for guidance, whether you realize it or not. Even if you haven't noticed them, someone younger than you is looking up to you, modeling their life after your own. There's a chance they may not even realize they're doing this. Whether consciously or subconsciously, someone is following in your footsteps, and you are responsible for the kind of influence you have on that person.

The most obvious instance of people we have an influence over are our children. I am both delighted and horrified daily to see my daughter imitate me.

When she snuggles up in a chair to read books, I know she learned that from me.

When she bows her head in prayer before meals, I know she learned that from me.

When she lashes out in anger, I know she also learned that from me.

I am growing more and more conscious of her watching eyes and her listening ears. They hold me accountable, and they remind me to use my influence over her for good. So we read the Bible at breakfast and quote Psalms in the bathtub. We go to church even when we're tired. We honor our parents (and grandparents) by spending time with them. We read "just one more story." And then one more.

Are we perfect? Far from it. I'm a sinner like everybody else, and I fail far more often than I would like to admit. But my tiny accountability partner is helping me grow into the person God created me to be.

Our own children are the most obvious people we influence, but even if you don't have children, you still have an influence on someone. People in your church. People at work. It doesn't even have to be someone younger than you; there are plenty of people who are younger than me whom I look up to greatly.

In the age of social media, our influence is likely greater than we think it is. Every post we create is making an impression on our friends and followers. You may think nobody is watching, but somebody is. It's time to stop being mindless about what we post on social media. Take a step back and look at what you're posting. Is it all about yourself? There's nothing wrong with posting about yourself; I love sharing pictures of my family and the things we're doing, and I know my family and friends enjoy keeping up with us in this way. But if everything I post is about me, I'm missing an opportunity that God has given me to be an influence.

Is using social media to be an influence for God effortless? Absolutely not! It's way easier to make social media all about ourselves. Using social media to share

God's truth requires us to be intentional. It requires us to put some thought into what we're going to say. It requires us to die to ourselves and our own selfish ambitions, believing that the greatest use of our voice is to proclaim God's truth. The reality is that more often than not, social media takes us away from the people God has placed in our lives to serve.

I enjoy social media just as much as the next person, maybe even more so. I was born in a world where there was no social media, but social media came on the scene before I was quite grown. I remember being an almost fifteen year old, elated that my parents had finally given me permission to create a Facebook account. Those early days of status updates and writing on friends' walls were pure fun and connection. I actually had to upload photos from my camera to the computer through a cable before I could even upload them to Facebook. Even in those days when I actually had to log into Facebook on a computer to use it, I recognized how much time I wasted there.

I didn't get a smart phone until I was twenty. Sometimes I wonder if I should have ever gotten one. I think the first thing I did on my new iPhone 4S was create an Instagram account. Those pretty little square photos captivated me. I'm not sure when my phone became so irresistible that I reached for it countless times every day without even thinking, but I'm acutely aware of it now. Social media is designed to suck us in. When you open social media, you may believe that you're a consumer enjoying a product, but the exact opposite is true. You are the product. Facebook is selling your attention to advertisers.

I'm not saying these things to tell you that you shouldn't be on social media. (Although maybe you shouldn't; this has to be a personal choice.) My hope is to encourage you to use social media intentionally. Be aware of its allure, but use it for God's glory to the best of your ability. I make very intentional, encouraging posts on social media. But I still have to be careful not to be taken in by the allure of the scroll. I want to use the influence God has given me for good. When we are faithful in selflessly using the influence we have, there's no limit to the influence God can give us.

Matthew 25:21
His lord said unto him, Well done, thou good and faithful servant: thou hast been faithful over a few things, I will make thee ruler over many things: enter thou into the joy of thy lord.

The people who have made the greatest difference in my life were not the ones who were seeking to make a name for themselves in influencing others; they were the ones who quietly served when nobody was watching. I think of Patsy Green, a retired missionary wife who welcomed me into her home multiple times as I wrestled with what God's will was for my life. She prayed with me and gave me counsel that kept me on the right path when God's will seemed unclear.

I think of Suza Rasmussen, a teacher in college. I had the privilege of being her secretary, but the greatest influence she had on my life didn't take place in the classroom or in the office; it happened over shared lunches as she counseled me through struggles, tears pouring down my face. It happened as she modeled to me what it meant to show hospitality by inviting me (and thousands of others) into her own home.

I think of my own mother who always put my needs before her own. She modeled to me what the sacrificial love of a mother looks like and she continues to model that love even though I've been out of the nest for nearly a decade. These women who have made such a difference in my life were all simply following the example Jesus set for us.

Matthew 20:28
Even as the Son of man came not to be ministered unto, but to minister, and to give his life a ransom for many.

We are all capable of following that same example and making a difference in the lives of those around us. The people of Nineveh, under the good influence of the king, had repented. They would soon learn that their repentant prayers had not fallen on deaf ears, and the change in their lives was well worth it.

QUESTIONS FOR DISCUSSION

1. Who has had a positive influence on your life?

2. Whom has God given you an influence over?

3. What does your social media use look like? Is it all about you, or is it about bringing glory to God?

4. Are you using your influence for good?

chapter Ten

FORGIVEN

Forgiveness undeserved
Granted from heaven.
I'll take God at His Word
And receive the gift He's given.

The people of Nineveh had repented, and God was
ready to show mercy.

> *Jonah 3:10*
> *And God saw their works, that they turned from*
> *their evil way; and God repented of the evil, that*
> *he had said that he would do unto them; and he*
> *did it not.*

This verse brings two questions to my mind. First,
when it says that "God repented," does this mean that
God changed His mind? Absolutely not! God was not

the One who had changed; it was the Ninevites who had changed. When they repented of their evil, God continued to act completely in character. It was never His intention to destroy a repentant city; His judgment was meant for the city that had not turned from its sin. When they changed, God remained His same merciful self, ready to forgive. This leads me to my second question: God repented of the evil when He saw their works. Does this mean that their salvation was a result of their good works? Not at all! But how do we know? Let's compare Scripture with Scripture to find an answer.

> Titus 3:5
> Not by works of righteousness which we have done, but according to his mercy he saved us, by the washing of regeneration, and renewing of the Holy Ghost;

The Bible specifically says that our salvation is not a result of works, but is the result of God's mercy and grace. So why is there this seeming discrepancy regarding the forgiveness of the city of Nineveh? It's true that God saw their works, but more importantly, He saw their hearts. Their works were a manifestation of the change in their hearts. When we accept Christ, the change He makes in our hearts should affect the way we live.

James 2:17-18
Even so faith, if it hath not works, is dead, being
alone. Yea, a man may say, Thou hast faith, and I
have works: shew me thy faith without thy works,
and I will shew thee my faith by my works.

Faith without works is dead, friends. I can tell you how much faith I have until I'm blue in the face, but unless my actions back it up, there's no proof that my faith is real. But what's the difference between works that demonstrate our faith and works based salvation?

Works based salvation is the belief that I have to do something in addition to accepting Jesus' finished work on the cross to be saved. Whether it's being baptized, attending church, tithing, or doing some good deed, faith in anything apart from Jesus means a lack of complete faith in Jesus. As a sophomore in college, I grappled with the question of whether or not I was really saved. A friend gave me an illustration that helped me answer that question.

Imagine a piece of paper with a line drawn down the middle. On one side, write all the good things you believe you may have done in your life that could qualify you for heaven. Praying a prayer, going to church, reading the Bible, being baptized, or, in my case, going to Bible college to prepare to be a missionary. On the other side of the paper write "Jesus." Then ask yourself, "What am I trusting? Am I trusting any of these good things I have written down? Or am I trusting

Jesus?" This isn't to say that you shouldn't be reading your Bible and going to church; you absolutely should! But reading your Bible and going to church will not save you from your sin. Only Jesus can do that. If you're trusting anything other than Jesus to save you, it's not enough. Only Jesus is enough.

When I asked myself that question on that warm November evening in Southern California, the answer was that I was trusting in a prayer I had prayed to save me. I was trusting in the fact that I was doing good works for God. I never realized that I couldn't do anything for God; anything good that I did was a result of His working through me. And it had to start with trusting in Jesus alone to save me. So that night, I asked God to forgive me. Because He is faithful and true to His word, He did! His forgiveness for me had nothing to do with how much I deserved it or if I prayed the right words; it had everything to do with His mercy and grace.

The Bible clearly teaches that salvation comes through faith alone, but my favorite Bible example of someone who Jesus saved that never did a single good thing to deserve it is the thief who died next to Him on the cross.

Luke 23:39-43
And one of the malefactors which were hanged railed on him, saying, If thou be Christ, save thyself and us. But the other answering rebuked him,

saying, Dost not thou fear God, seeing thou art in the same condemnation? And we indeed justly; for we receive the due reward of our deeds: but this man hath done nothing amiss. And he said unto Jesus, Lord, remember me when thou comest into thy kingdom. And Jesus said unto him, Verily I say unto thee, To day shalt thou be with me in paradise.

He never had the chance to be baptized. He never went to church a day in his life. He didn't personally share the gospel with anyone. He died the death that he deserved as a criminal. Jesus forgave him anyway, and he is spending eternity in heaven today. But I can guarantee you that if the thief on the cross had lived to have the chance, his life would have reflected the change God had made in his heart.

There are so many people today who claim that they are Christians, but their lives don't back it up.

Titus 1:16
They profess that they know God; but in works they deny him, being abominable, and disobedient, and unto every good work reprobate.

Matthew 7:20
Wherefore by their fruits ye shall know them.

Does this mean that every Christian will do what's good and right one hundred percent of the time? Of course not. Since coming to know Christ, I have failed time and time again to live the way I know He wants me to live. Sanctification, the process of becoming holy, is just that: a process. It's a slow process, and sometimes it's a painful one. Sometimes it feels like I take one step forward and two steps back. But when I look back on my life with Christ these last seven years, I can see progress. I see growth.

2 Peter 3:18
But grow in grace, and in the knowledge of our Lord and Saviour Jesus Christ. To him be glory both now and for ever. Amen.

But if works don't save us, why bother? Why spend our lives doing good when Jesus has already done everything necessary for our salvation? Shouldn't we just get to do what we want now? Paul gives a great answer to this in Ephesians.

Ephesians 2:8-10
For by grace are ye saved through faith; and that not of yourselves: it is the gift of God: not of works, lest any man should boast. For we are his workmanship, created in Christ Jesus unto good works, which God hath before ordained that we should walk in them.

First of all, Paul reiterates the fact that we are not saved by works; we are saved by our faith in Jesus and the work He has done on the cross. But if God's only desire for our lives was to redeem us from our sin, He would take us to heaven the minute we believed. He has left us on earth because He has a purpose for our lives here, and that purpose is to do good in His name. He desires that we would represent Him well as His ambassadors, fulfilling the purpose for which He created. God has given us talents and abilities that He desires us to use for Him. When we consider all He has done for us, why would we not live our lives for Him?

The people of Nineveh sincerely repented from the heart, and their works were an outward demonstration of their faith. How can we know they were sincere? We can't. But God knew. He sees the heart. And when He saw the sincere repentance of their hearts, demonstrated by their works, He was ready to forgive. What a beautiful story of redemption! And Jonah was there to witness it all! But was he happy about it? Not in the least.

QUESTIONS FOR DISCUSSION

1. What are you trusting to save you? Works, or faith in Jesus?

2. Are the works in your life an outward reflection of the change Jesus has made on the inside?

3. If the answer to the above question was "no," what needs to change?

chapter eleven

WHEN LIFE'S NOT FAIR

Jesus has overcome
Death and the grave.
The victory He won,
And the way for me He paved.

Jonah 4:1
But it displeased Jonah exceedingly, and he was
very angry.

God had granted extravagant forgiveness to the people of Nineveh, but Jonah, the prophet of God, was actually angry! What was this guy's problem? How did he not get the point by now? In his anger, he prayed to God once more. What a stark contrast between his prayer from the whale's belly and his prayer here.

Jonah 4:2
And he prayed unto the Lord, and said, I pray thee,
O Lord, was not this my saying, when I was yet in
my country? Therefore I fled before unto Tarshish:
for I knew that thou art a gracious God, and mer-
ciful, slow to anger, and of great kindness, and re-
pentest thee of the evil.

Oh, right. I see the problem now. Jonah was angry because God had done exactly what Jonah knew He would do, knowing that He was a God of forgiveness. That's why He ran away from God in the first place: he didn't want those dirty, rotten sinners in Nineveh to get a second chance.

Jonah 4:3
Therefore now, O Lord, take, I beseech thee, my life
from me; for it is better for me to die than to live.

A bit dramatic, don't you think? But Jonah was dead serious (no pun intended). He actually wanted God to take his life because he didn't think it was worth living in a world where God forgave sinners. But do you see the irony? God had just given a second chance to Jonah, the rebellious prophet who tried to run from His very presence. Why should He not give a second chance to the people of Nineveh as well? He responded with the patience that is so very true to His nature.

Jonah 4:4
Then said the Lord, Doest thou well to be angry?

He simply asks a question. He assumes Jonah is a pretty smart guy; surely he can see how nonsensical it is for him to be angry when he was just as much in need of God's mercy as the people in Nineveh. But Jonah doesn't give an answer.

Jonah 4:5
So Jonah went out of the city, and sat on the east side of the city, and there made him a booth, and sat under it in the shadow, till he might see what would become of the city.

Instead of answering God's question, Jonah storms out of the city like a pouting child stomping into his room and slamming the door. He makes a shelter for himself, and watches to see what's going to happen to Nineveh. Can you believe this guy? God had already said He was going to show mercy, but Jonah still expected fire and brimstone to rain down on Nineveh. Not only did he expect it, he was looking forward to the show.

We look at Jonah and shake our heads, but have we ever been guilty of the same thing? Have we seen people around us living in wickedness, but it seems like God is blessing them abundantly? Meanwhile, we're His children, and we seem to face hardship after hardship. Shouldn't He make our lives just a little easier? Don't we deserve it? Fortunately, God doesn't dole out blessings based on a scale of merit, just as He doesn't give salvation based on works. And He wants us to have the same mindset that He does.

Matthew 5:43-45
Ye have heard that it hath been said, Thou shalt love thy neighbour, and hate thine enemy. But I say unto you, Love your enemies, bless them that curse you, do good to them that hate you, and pray for them which despitefully use you, and persecute you; that ye may be the children of your Father which is in heaven: for he maketh his sun to rise on the evil and on the good, and sendeth rain on the just and on the unjust.

Love your enemies. We've heard it before, but do we really live it? Jonah didn't. But if we really want to be like our Father, God, we must. We are called to be busy loving and serving others, trusting all the while that God will take care of us. But even as we trust Him to take care of us, we must accept that He allows good and bad, sunshine and rain, into the lives of the unrepentant sinner as well as the saint who is justified by the blood of His Son.

Job 2:10
But he said unto her, Thou speakest as one of the

foolish women speaketh. What? shall we receive
good at the hand of God, and shall we not receive
evil? In all this did not Job sin with his lips.

Does the way God works in our lives always make
sense to us? Not at all. But if God always made sense,
would He really be God? And do I really want Him to
give me what I deserve?

Romans 6:23
For the wages of sin is death; but the gift of God is
eternal life through Jesus Christ our Lord.

What do I really deserve? Death. Eternal separation from God. The fact that He sent Jesus to give me
eternal life is a gift far beyond my comprehension.
Anything good He gives me in addition to salvation is
just a bonus. When I stop to think about it, He really
has done so much good in my life.

Romans 8:32
He that spared not his own Son, but delivered him
up for us all, how shall he not with him also freely
give us all things?

But what about the things that we perceive to be
bad things? So many of the heartaches in this world
can simply be attributed to the results of sin.

Romans 5:12
Wherefore, as by one man sin entered into the

world, and death by sin; and so death passed upon
all men, for that all have sinned:

Sin entered into the world, and the whole world was cursed. Everything that was or would be started down a path of death and decay. The bad news is, things are not going to get better.

2 Timothy 3:13
But evil men and seducers shall wax worse and
worse, deceiving, and being deceived.

Evil is not going anywhere as long as we are on this sin-cursed earth. But thankfully that's not the end of the story. Even in the middle of this mess called life, we have a reason to smile.

John 16:33
These things I have spoken unto you, that in me
ye might have peace. In the world ye shall have
tribulation: but be of good cheer; I have overcome
the world.

Jesus has overcome!

When the cancer diagnosis comes, we can be confident He has overcome.

When a miscarriage breaks our hearts, we can be confident He has overcome.

When the relationship is broken, we can be confident He has overcome.

When the dream job is lost, we can be confident He has overcome.

When an accident changes our lives, we can be confident He has overcome.

When the life of a loved one is cut short, we can be confident He has overcome.

Through Him, we can always overcome. We don't have to look with envy on those we believe are less deserving than we are of God's goodness. We are called to love them, serve them, and show them who God is through our lives. Sometimes God allows us to go through these difficult times so that He can use our testimony to reach others. My friend Rebecca is allowing the Lord to use her difficult testimony in such a way. Even through the storm in her life, her testimony points straight to the One who has overcome. I want to share her story with you in her words.

I wanted to be on fire for the Lord. I truly did. And while I was looking for something to start that fire, God lit it for me. Unfortunately it was in the form of stage 3 adenocarcinoma. Did you know that esophageal cancer is one of the deadliest forms of cancer there is? I didn't. But He saw me through it. The chemo, the radiation, the surgery. He saw me through it all.

Then nine months after my esophagectomy, I was diagnosed with cancer again. This time it was in my lungs, liver, and there was a cancerous mass growing on my spine. It had crushed my vertebrae and was pushing on my spinal cord. But shortly before this diagnosis the Lord had led me to the book of Jonah. I had opened my Bible one day and was praying that He would speak to me. It was a new Bible, a King James Cross Reference version and I hadn't explored all the extra pages yet. One was titled, "God Promises to Show You What to Do." In the verses listed was Jonah 2:2. It reads:

And said, I cried by reason of mine affliction unto the Lord, and he heard me; out of the belly of hell cried I, and thou heardest my voice.

I already knew something was wrong from the amount of pain I was in from my back. At that point though the doctors were hoping it was just a fracture. But I felt the Lord leading me to read Jonah. It is a much different account than the one we are given as children in Sunday School. It ends with Jonah vowing to be angry even unto death. But why? Why would this prophet, this man of God, choose to be so angry instead of rejoicing with the Ninevites in their decision to turn toward the Lord? I believe that the Lord was using this portion of Scripture to prepare my heart not to be angry and to help prepare the hearts of my husband and children as well. If He decides to take me, it won't be His will for just my life, but theirs as well. So regardless of how much time I have left I will not spend it angry. I will spend it rejoicing.

Even when God allows us to go through the fire, we can trust that He is still taking care of us. Even in the midst of the storm, we can have confidence.

Romans 8:37
Nay, in all these things we are more than conquerors through him that loved us.

More than conquerors, friends. But was Jonah living his life as a conqueror? Not at all. Yet God continued to show His complete love and mercy for this wayward prophet.

QUESTIONS FOR DISCUSSION

1. Have you ever felt that life wasn't fair?

2. What circumstance have you overcome through Christ?

3. How can you show God's love to others, even in the midst of your own trials?

4. Are you willing to let God use your testimony, even the difficult parts? What is one practical way you could do this?

chapter Twelve

GOD PREPARED

God cares for me
By whatever means
He divinely sees
My soul most needs.

Jonah had stormed off to his metaphorical room, and God had had enough.

Oh wait, that's not how the story goes. Jonah had stormed off to his metaphorical room, and God showed mercy to him once again.

Time for a little confession. I was one of those kids who dealt with anger by storming off to my room and slamming the door. My mother has often recounted the repetitive story of little Michelle storming off to her room and declaring, "I'm never eating again!" Did my mom say, "Fine. I'm holding you to that, and I'm never providing food for you again."? Of course not.

Loving parents take care of their children, even when their children are acting like, well, children. And how often must God see us as children who just don't know any better?

> *Jonah 4:6*
> *And the Lord God prepared a gourd, and made it to come up over Jonah, that it might be a shadow over his head, to deliver him from his grief. So Jonah was exceeding glad of the gourd.*

God saw poor, pathetic Jonah sitting out in the Middle Eastern heat, and He had compassion on him. He wanted to give Jonah another chance to see just how amazing His grace was. So he caused a plant to miraculously grow up and give Jonah shade. This is the first time we see Jonah happy in the entire book. Did he finally get it? Did he finally get that God was trying to teach him a lesson about His love? Was he glad because of whom he finally saw God to be?

No. He was glad because of the gourd. He was happy about the thing that was contributing to his immediate comfort. We're quick to judge him as foolish, but don't we do the same thing?

God was trying to get Jonah's attention, but Jonah just didn't get it. He was once again in a position of discomfort, and he just wasn't sure that this life was worth living anymore. But he wasn't the first prophet to despair of life in the desert.

Elijah was a faithful and bold prophet under the reign of the wicked King Ahab. Because of the wickedness of Ahab, God had caused a drought and a famine in the land. He showed His power through Elijah by sending fire down from heaven to consume Elijah's sacrifice, while the false prophets of Baal cried out for fire in vain. The false prophets were then killed. Immediately following this victory, God sent rain. Elijah had been a faithful messenger and allowed God to show His glory through him. But not everyone was pleased.

1 Kings 19:1-2
And Ahab told Jezebel all that Elijah had done, and withal how he had slain all the prophets with the sword. Then Jezebel sent a messenger unto Elijah, saying, So let the gods do to me, and more also, if I make not thy life as the life of one of them by to morrow morning.

Elijah had done what God had commanded him, but he found that his life was in jeopardy. It is under these circumstances that we find him despairing of life, just as Jonah did years later.

1 Kings 19:4
But he himself went a day's journey into the wilderness, and came and sat down under a juniper tree: and he requested for himself that he might die; and

said, It is enough; now, O Lord, take away my life;
for I am not better than my fathers.

He had done the right thing, but it still seemed that he was facing bad consequences. Yet in his despair, God showed His great love for Elijah.

1 Kings 19:5-8
And as he lay and slept under a juniper tree, be-
hold, then an angel touched him, and said unto
him, Arise and eat. And he looked, and, behold,
there was a cake baken on the coals, and a cruse
of water at his head. And he did eat and drink, and
laid him down again. And the angel of the Lord
came again the second time, and touched him, and
said, Arise and eat; because the journey is too great
for thee. And he arose and did eat and drink, and
went in the strength of that meat forty days and
forty nights unto Horeb the mount of God.

God saw him where he was and provided exactly what he needed to be strengthened and encouraged. God's goal for Elijah was the same as His goal for Jonah. He wanted to conform both of them to His image, and He did so in the way that they each needed at the time. Elijah needed His gentleness. We see that in the following verses.

1 Kings 19:9-10
And he came thither unto a cave, and lodged there;

and, behold, the word of the Lord came to him, and he said unto him, What doest thou here, Elijah? And he said, I have been very jealous for the Lord God of hosts: for the children of Israel have forsaken thy covenant, thrown down thine altars, and slain thy prophets with the sword; and I, even I am left; and they seek my life, to take it away.

God gives Elijah a chance to voice his grievance, and it seems that he has a legitimate cause to be upset. He had done the right thing, but life was still not going the way he thought it should. From this position of grief, God revealed Himself to Elijah in the way that he needed to see Him: as a kind, loving God.

1 Kings 19:11-12
And he said, Go forth, and stand upon the mount before the Lord. And, behold, the Lord passed by, and a great and strong wind rent the mountains, and brake in pieces the rocks before the Lord; but the Lord was not in the wind: and after the wind an earthquake; but the Lord was not in the earthquake: and after the earthquake a fire; but the Lord was not in the fire: and after the fire a still small voice.

God showed His strength in His gentleness, and this caused Elijah to take heart. Elijah's circumstances had not changed, but he knew that even if he had to come against strength that compared to wind, earth-quakes, or fire, the quiet strength that he had in the Lord was stronger. He went forth from this encounter with God and continued his ministry with courage. God continued to protect him, and eventually he was caught up into heaven in a chariot of fire. He was one of two people mentioned in the Bible that did not actually die.

God will always prepare and place in our lives the things that will draw us to Him and make us into the people He wants us to be. God had tried to reveal Himself to Jonah through His tender care by providing the gourd, but Jonah still didn't get it. His focus was on the comfort of the gourd rather than the God Who made the gourd.

In first world countries, we've grown attached to our comforts. Air conditioning. Grocery stores. Ready made clothing. Restaurants. The list could go on and on. God has given us far more than we deserve. But what happens when we forget that these blessings come from Him in the first place? What happens when we try to find our happiness in the gift rather than in the giver?

Jonah 4:7
But God prepared a worm when the morning rose the next day, and it smote the gourd that it withered.

God wanted to show Jonah His love, but when Jonah still didn't recognize that love, God sent a worm to eat away the gourd that He had just allowed to grow. God wasn't trying to supply physical comfort for Jonah; God was trying to make Jonah into the person He wanted him to be, and He wasn't going to stop until His mission was accomplished.

The gourd and the worm weren't the first things God had prepared for Jonah, nor would they be the last things.

Jonah 1:17
Now the Lord had prepared a great fish to swallow up Jonah. And Jonah was in the belly of the fish three days and three nights.

God had prepared the fish for the same purpose of conforming Jonah to His image. You would think that that experience would have gotten his attention. In fact, it looked like it did. But Jonah was quick to return to his old, cynical ways. The book of Jonah mentions one last thing that God prepared.

Jonah 4:8
And it came to pass, when the sun did arise, that God prepared a vehement east wind; and the sun beat upon the head of Jonah, that he fainted, and wished in himself to die, and said, It is better for me to die than to live.

Jonah wasn't in a position where he needed to see the comfort of God's still small voice. The time had come for God to get his attention through the wind. In a last ditch effort to get Jonah's attention, God sent a harsh Middle Eastern wind to make things quite uncomfortable for Jonah. I don't know what climate you live in, but if you've never experienced a sand storm in the desert, count your blessings.

I had the privilege of living in the desert for four years while I was in college. The privilege was the incredible college I attended, not the desert in which it was located. Harsh, hot winds were a part of everyday life. Gusts of twenty miles per hour were not uncommon. I remember many nights in which I spent more time than I ever wanted to spend washing sand out of my ears and eyebrows. It's like a day at the beach, only there's no water and you're not dressed for a day at the beach. These little dust storms were an annoyance, but sometimes sand storms can be more than an annoyance. They can be dangerous.

In the spring of 2013, we experienced a sand storm that was far worse than anything many of the locals could remember in their lifetimes. Winds clocked in at seventy miles per hour. Walking outside was a challenge. Sand was everywhere. Evening classes were cancelled. They posted signs that students were not to leave campus; the driving conditions were extremely dangerous. Sixteen vehicles were reportedly involved in accidents due to that storm, resulting in two people being injured. Unfortunately, they didn't post the warning signs before I left campus to take a friend to a job interview at the mall eleven miles away. God protected us on that drive, I have no doubt. There was only one point I was fearful that we had set ourselves up for catastrophe. We had almost made it safely back to campus when we reached a stretch of road where there was zero visibility due to the sand. Looking through the windshield, it appeared as if we were driving underground. We were safe from the blasting sand in the little cocoon of my tiny Honda Civic, but Jonah was left exposed to the elements. I can only imagine his misery.

The Hebrew word from which "fainted" is translated in this verse means "to cover." Jonah tried to cover himself from the harsh elements, realized the futility of it, and wished once more that he could die. God had done everything He could to get Jonah's attention. So, did He finally leave Jonah alone? I mean, this guy just can't seem to get the point!

How about you? Do you get it? What's the point of this whole story anyway?

QUESTIONS FOR DISCUSSION

1. Is your focus on the things that bring you comfort, or on the God Who provides those things?

2. Describe a time in your life when God did something to show how much He cares for you.

3. What would need to happen for God to conform you to His image? Is His tender care enough? Or does He need to take your comfort?

chapter Thirteen

MYSELF LAST

When I put myself last,
I can finally be free.
On God my cares I cast,
And He takes care of me.

After all Jonah had gone through, he still didn't get the point. God, in His compassion, takes the time to try to spell things out for Jonah.

Jonah 4:9
And God said to Jonah, Doest thou well to be angry for the gourd? And he said, I do well to be angry, even unto death.

At least Jonah is sticking to his guns on this one. God took the gourd that had given him so much happiness and comfort. He was angry, and he believed with his whole heart that he had the right to be angry, so much so that he really did wish he could die. What a stubborn man.

So what's the point of the whole story? Is it a happy little Sunday school story about a man being swallowed by a fish? Is it about God's love for a lost, wicked city that He then forgave? There are lessons to be learned from each of these elements of the story, but if we think those things are the whole point of the story, we're sorely mistaken.

Jonah 4:10-11
Then said the Lord, Thou hast had pity on the gourd, for the which thou hast not laboured, neither madest it grow, which came up in a night, and perished in a night. And should not I spare Nineveh, that great city, wherein are more than sixscore thousand persons that cannot discern between their right hand and their left hand; and also much cattle?

Jonah had pity on the gourd, and he hadn't even made the gourd!

What? Of course he hadn't made the gourd! People can't just make gourds! So who had made the gourd? God did. And yet He didn't really care that much about it. He was busy caring about something else. God hadn't just made the gourd; He had made the people of Nineveh. If Jonah cared so much about something he hadn't even made, how much more did God care about the people that He had made? More than 120,000 of those people couldn't even tell their right from their left just yet. Because they were children. God's children. He loved them. He would send His own Son to die for them. He cared for those little individuals and knew every detail about them, right down to the number of hairs on their heads.

Matthew 10:29-31
Are not two sparrows sold for a farthing? and one
of them shall not fall on the ground without your
Father. But the very hairs of your head are all num-
bered. Fear ye not therefore, ye are of more value
than many sparrows.

God placed incredible value on these little ones. But if Jonah didn't, maybe he would care about the cattle. Not because cows are so cute; people in Bible times didn't think like that. To Jonah, cattle represented wealth. God said to Jonah, "If you don't care about the people, do you at least care to spare the wealth of Nineveh?" That's just how shallow Jonah was acting.

But what was God really trying to do here? He was trying to show Jonah just how much He loved people. And maybe Jonah would put two and two together and realize that he was a person too.

The book of Jonah is not the story of Jonah and the whale or Jonah and Nineveh; it's the story of God and His love for people, the story of God doing what He does best and offering His love and forgiveness to heathen sailors, a wicked city, and a wayward prophet. From the very beginning when God called Jonah to Nineveh, He cared about every person in the equation. He wanted Jonah, as His servant, to put the needs of others before his own needs. Jonah could trust God to meet his needs, but he never quite seemed to see how God was taking care of him all along. God sent a storm on the sea to get his attention, but that didn't work. He prepared a fish to swallow him, and that seemed like it got Jonah's attention. So God gave Jonah a second chance. Jonah did the right thing, but perhaps he had the wrong motivation. He proved once more that his heart was in the wrong place as he awaited the destruction of Nineveh. So God kept trying to get Jonah's attention in whatever way He could. He prepared a gourd, a worm, and a wind. All because He wanted to show Jonah that He cared.

I don't know about you, but I can certainly see myself in Jonah. I've often missed the point in all that God has led me to do in my life. As He's led me through three cross country moves, as I became a wife and then a mother, as I experienced death and tragedy in my life, I've missed the point. Everything God has allowed to happen in my life, whether it was good or bad in my eyes, was to draw me closer to Him and to make me more like Him. And being more like Him means being willing to sacrifice myself for the needs of others. Everything God allows into my life has a holy purpose.

> *Romans 8:28-29*
> *And we know that all things work together for good to them that love God, to them who are the called according to his purpose. For whom he did foreknow, he also did predestinate to be conformed to the image of his Son, that he might be the first-born among many brethren.*

Romans 8:28 is a common verse shared with people who are going through hard times, and it can certainly be an encouragement in trials. But it applies to literally everything that happens to us as believers. All things work together for good. It's a shame that verse 29 isn't more often quoted with verse 28. Maybe that's because we shy away from words like *foreknow* and *predestinate.* To get over our fear of Bible words, it helps to define them.

Foreknow means, "to be aware of an event before it happens." So when we say that God "foreknew" who would be saved, it doesn't mean He picked and chose who would be saved; we all have a choice. God can't help knowing what that choice will be because He's God, and He knows everything.

When we define *foreknow* it makes the word *predestinate* less scary. Predestinate means, "to determine an outcome or course of events in advance by divine will." Did God determine ahead of time whether or not we would be saved? No, He just foreknew that. What He determined in advance was that for those who did choose to be saved, He would do everything He possibly could to conform us to the image of Jesus.

Now think back to verse 28: all things work together for good. What greater good is there in my life than that I would be more like Jesus and have a closer relationship with Him? When I see that this is the purpose of everything God causes or allows in my life, whether it be good or bad in my eyes, it puts things in perspective. God was trying to make Jonah more like Himself.

The narrative about Jonah in the Bible ends with God's question to him regarding whether or not He should have spared Nineveh. After all, He spared Jonah time and time again. It would seem that the story ends with Jonah never really learning his lesson, but I've got good news: he did learn his lesson. How do I know? Because he was the one who wrote down the story. The book doesn't explicitly tell us that Jonah was the author, but he was the only one who could have known all the details well enough to write it. He didn't bother putting himself in the best light when writing the book; he told the hard facts, his failures and all. Why would someone so self-centered tell such a self-deprecating story? Because he finally learned his lesson about selfishness. He finally learned to put others before himself. And the people he chose to put before himself were you and I.

Jonah wrote his story, and God allowed it to be preserved so that we could learn a lesson that Jonah had to learn the hard way. It's a story of learning to lose yourself in service to others, but it's wrapped in the hope that you just might find an unexplainable joy along the way. As you're busy serving others, you can count on God to take care of you. He loves the world, but the world is made up of individual people. He loves those individual people with an everlasting love. It took me longer than I like to admit to realize that I'm a person too.

I was passionate about telling the whole world of God's love for them, but I was in my second year of Bible college before I really understood God's love for me. He foreknew that I would understand His love and accept the gift that He gave me in His Son, and so He determined beforehand the ways that He would conform me to the image of His Son. Even after accepting His gift of salvation, there were still many times that I pushed against the things that He was doing in my life to accomplish His ultimate purpose. I'm still altogether too prone to pushing back, but I'm learning more and more to look at the big picture.

1 Corinthians 13:11-12
When I was a child, I spake as a child, I understood as a child, I thought as a child: but when I became

a man, I put away childish things. For now we see
through a glass, darkly; but then face to face: now
I know in part; but then shall I know even as also
I am known.

When we are new believers, children in the faith, many things seem a little unclear to us. The Bible says it's like looking through a glass, or in a mirror. The mirrors in the time that this passage was written would have been made from steel, not from glass. I can't imagine you would get a very accurate reflection of anything in a steel mirror. But the day is coming when we will see God face to face. We will finally know everything about Him, just as He already knows everything about us. What a day that will be!

But until that day, we will continue in our quest for understanding, getting to know Him better and better through His Word. And we will submit to His refining fire as He does everything He possibly can to conform us to His image. Because even when we can't see what God is doing, we can trust He is at work for our good.

Job 23:8-10
Behold, I go forward, but he is not there; and back-
ward, but I cannot perceive him: on the left hand,
where he doth work, but I cannot behold him: he
hideth himself on the right hand, that I cannot see
him: but he knoweth the way that I take: when he
hath tried me, I shall come forth as gold.

QUESTIONS FOR DISCUSSION

1. What do I care about more than I care about people?

2. In what area am I tempted to put myself first?

3. What one thing can I do today to put someone else's needs above my own?

CONCLUSION

God has blessed me with what I believe is the best writing spot in the world. Every Friday I get to sip white mochas on the second floor of a coffee shop in a beautiful, old brick building. I sit in front of a large square window that reaches almost to the ceiling and enjoy the incredible view. The sight of the Chattanooga skyline takes my breath away every single time.

On my drive to the coffee shop, I crest a hill and see the Walnut Street Bridge. My heart quickens at the sight of this beautiful pedestrian bridge. It's a focal point of our beautiful scenic skyline. As I sit for hours writing and periodically gazing out the window at the skyline, I see so much beauty that was made by man. In addition to the bridge, I see the iconic pointed glass rooftop of our aquarium. I see a little golden horse peeking over the trees, marking the location of a carousel filled with hand-carved wooden animals. I see the art museum in the distance. I think of the incredible masterpieces within its walls.

And then I see the tree covered mountain looming in the distance. God's creation, breathtaking in every sense of the word. I love my city. But when God looks at my city, He's not looking so much at the beautiful architecture, or even the mountains and trees that He formed. If I take a closer look, I can see what He *is* looking at.

He's looking at the people taking their Friday afternoon walk on the pedestrian bridge. Each one with a story, each one with a dream, each one with an eternal soul. I see them walk by, but they sometimes blend into the scenery. Strangely, the people sitting at the table right next to me in the coffee shop begin to blend into the scenery as well. I sit in my own little world, writing, doing this work that I know is so important. But maybe I'm missing the point.

What's far more important than my comfortable quiet spot with my lavender white mocha in hand is the girl downstairs who makes that lavender white mocha for me every single week. What's important is the relationship I've built with her over these weeks. What matters is how I'm using my words to show God's love to the people I cross paths with every single day.

If my focus is on myself, on my own little routines and rhythms, I will never have the joy that I long for. I will live an unfulfilled life. But when I look up from my little world and notice the needs of others, that's when the joyful life begins.

Nobody knows how to communicate a felt need quite the way a toddler does in the middle of the night. Pro tip: never ask a parent how their child is sleeping. The answer is likely that they're not. My toddler still wakes frequently, and this night waking is something I have struggled with for her entire life. But God is teaching me a very real lesson, even in this.

I like sleep. I *need* sleep. Physically, we cannot survive without sleep. I have woken up many mornings after a mostly sleepless night completely convinced that I would not be able to survive the day. People can't survive on this little sleep! But somehow I have survived every day. In fact, I'm beginning to thrive. The reason is not that I'm getting more sleep, although that has improved a little. I believe I could have thrived all along if I had just learned this lesson sooner.

When I stop thinking of myself, stop thinking of how much sleep I'm getting (or losing), and focus on the very real need my daughter has for comfort, God takes care of me. When I lose myself in a life of service, I find the true joy I have been after all this time.

Are you asleep to the needs of others? It's time to wake up and see the needs around you. Do what you can to meet those needs. Trust that God will take care of you. Because He will. And when you lose yourself, you will finally find real joy.

ACKNOWLEDGEMENTS

My first book took two-and-a-half years to write; this one took five months. The difference between the two was the amount of support I allowed into my life. My name may be on the cover, but this book is the result of the effort and influence of many.

To the wonderful people at hope*writers, thank you for giving me the tools I needed to write meaningful words without sacrificing my meaningful life and to serve my readers well.

To the incredible people at Stone Cup Cafe, thank you for keeping me caffeinated and providing a quiet place to write.

Kassie, you were my cheerleader every step of the way. Thank you for listening to my rambling and celebrating the little victories.

Christina, Priscilla, and Rebecca, thank you for letting me share your stories. It has been a privilege to watch God do a work in and through your lives.

Angela and Bethany, thank you for the gift of your

editing skills. I write few words that don't pass through your filter first, and for that I am incredibly grateful.

Mom and Dad, thank you for encouraging me and for being willing to dig in to help me make my writing the best it can possibly be.

To my church family at Life Gate Baptist Church, thank you for your encouragement and support as the Lord has led me in this ministry of writing.

Baby Angela, you are the most content child in the whole world. Thank you for being patient with me as I worked on this project. You may be two years old, but you'll always be my baby.

Cute Steve, you gave me the time that I needed to put these words on paper. You vacuumed the house, napped the baby, and sacrificed sleep of your own. I could not have done it without you. I love you so much.

To the God of Jonah who is my God as well, thank you for not only giving me a second chance at life, but also a second chance to write a book for Your glory. Thank you for revealing Yourself to us through written words, my favorite thing in the world. I pray that I have rightly divided those words in a way that will point others to You.

BIBLIOGRAPHY

Deane, W.J., et. al. "Jonah." *The Pulpit Commentary,* edited by H.D.M. Spence and Joseph S. Exell, Vol. 14, WM. B. Eerdmans Publishing Company, 1977, pp. 1-102.

Fink, Paul R. "Jonah." *Liberty Bible Commentary,* edited by Jerry Falwell, Vol. 1, Old-Time Gospel Hour, 1982, pp. 1723-1733.

Livingston, G. Herbert. "Jonah." *The Wycliffe Bible Commentary,* edited by Charles F. Pfeiffer, The Moody Bible Institute, 1962, pp. 843-850.

ABOUT THE AUTHOR

Michelle Elaine Burton is a youth pastor's wife and the mom of a beautiful two-year-old daughter. She is the author of *Seasons of Change: God's Faithfulness in the Life of Ruth.* She has a Bachelor's Degree in Bible from West Coast Baptist College. Michelle lives with her family and their hamsters in Chattanooga, TN. You can find more of her writing at michelleelaineburton.com. You can also connect with Michelle on Instagram at @MichelleElaineBurton.

Seasons of Change: God's Faithfulness in the Life of Ruth

When life doesn't go how you hoped, dreamed or planned...

- Does God still have a plan?
- Is He still faithful?
- Does He still care?

In this verse by verse study on the book of Ruth, you will be encouraged in your faith as you navigate the ever-changing seasons of your own life. As you draw parallels between Ruth's experiences and your own, you will be strengthened with the confidence that the same God who was crafting Ruth's story has a good plan for your life. No matter what circumstances you are facing, there is truly no limit to how God can use your story, just as He is using the story of Ruth thousands of years later.

Available on Amazon.

The 60 Second Quiet Time

A beginner's guide to having a daily time with God

To create lasting routines, it's vital to start small. This guide to a Sixty Second Quiet Time will help you create a daily time with the Lord that will be a catalyst for a lifelong walk with Him.

In busier seasons of life, this tool will help you keep your walk with God a priority and find calm amidst the chaos.

Maybe you already have an established time with God, but you need a quick way to refocus in the afternoon. This guide is for you too!

You can download this free guide at
https://michelleelaineburton.com/quiet-time/

Made in USA - Crawfordsville, IN
20229_9781736007921
03.02.2022 1337